Study Guide to

The Bluest Eye
by Toni Morrison

by Ray Moore

Toni Morrison speaking at "A Tribute to Chinua Achebe - 50 Years Anniversary of *Things Fall Apart*." The Town Hall, New York City, February 26th, 2008. Photograph by Angela Radulescu.

Contents

Acknowledgements:

I am indebted to the work of numerous critics as I have acknowledged in the Bibliography. As always, I stand on the shoulders of giants. Where I am conscious of having taken an idea or a phrase from a particular author, I have cited the source in the text. Any failure to do so is an omission which I will immediately correct if it is drawn to my attention. I believe that all quotations used fall under the definition of 'fair use.' If I am in error on any quotation, I will immediately correct if it is drawn to my attention.

Thanks are due to my wife, Barbara, for reading the manuscript, offering valuable suggestions, and for putting the text into the correct formats for publication. Any errors which remain are my own

Preface

A Study Guide is an *aid* to the close reading of a text; it is *never* a substitute for reading the text. This novel deserves to be read *reflectively*, and the aim of this guide is to facilitate such a reading. The study guide questions have *no* answers provided. This is a deliberate choice. I am writing for readers who want to come to *their own conclusions* about the text and not simply to be told what to think about it by someone else. Even 'suggested' answers would limit the *exploration of the text* by readers themselves which is my primary aim.

In the classroom, I found that students frequently came up with answers that I had not even considered, and, not infrequently, that they expressed their ideas better than I could have done. The point of this Guide is to *open up* the text, not to close it down by providing 'ready-made answers.

Spoiler alert!

If you are reading the novel for the first time, you may wish to go straight to the Study Guide and Questions section and come back to the introductory sections later since they do explain everything that happens in the novel, including the ending!

Introduction

Plot Summary

The story is set in the black community of Lorain, Ohio, in 1941. The narrator, Claudia (who was nine years old at the time) tells the tragic story of her friend, Pecola, who was eleven. Other narrative voices (including a third person narrator) fill in parts of the story that Claudia could not know. Pecola's family is by 1941 dysfunctional: her father drinks heavily and her mother spends most of her time at the house of a rich white family where she is housekeeper. Her parents' quarrels are violent affairs.

Pecola, a particularly passive person, thus grows up in a loveless and violent house. Convinced that being black makes her ugly, and that her life will never improve until she is perceived by others as beautiful, she prays fervently for blue eyes. Events culminate in her rape by her own father after which she has a complete mental breakdown convinced that her eyes have miraculously turned to the bluest blue.

Why Read this Book?

Toni Morrison won the Nobel Prize in Literature in 1993. She is one of the most important American writers in the post-World War II period. More than this, she is a strong voice for African Americans and for women.

Anyone who does not understand the pervasiveness of white values in American culture and how destructive this can be to black people's sense of their own identity needs to read this book

Important: Issues with this Book

This novel was not written for young adults; it was written for adults. Morrison includes beautifully written descriptions of a woman's feelings when she makes love (and achieves orgasm) with a man she loves and an uncompromising description of the rape of an eleven-year-old girl. Morrison herself has described the novel as "a terrible story about things one would rather not know anything about" (quoted by Malmgren, Bloom. Ed. *Interpretations Updated* 153).

That said, I know that the novel has been set for use in high school (12th grade), and it is certainly the sort of novel that young adults *should* read, discuss and study.

Dramatis Personæ: List of Significant Characters

The MacTeer Family and Associates

Mr. MacTeer does not appear much in the narrative mainly because he works long, hard hours to keep the family housed, fed and clothed. He is, however, fiercely protective of his daughters.

Mrs. MacTeer is a strict disciplinarian who is not averse to giving her daughters a whipping when she considers that they need it. She also has a quick temper and a tendency to 'fuss'. Nevertheless, her children know that she loves them and is genuinely concerned for their well-being.

Claudia MacTeer is the adult narrator of parts of the novel and its true protagonist. Nine years old in 1941 when the main incidents take place, she is Pecola's friend. As a black child proud of her color, she rebels against the white ideal of beauty that pervades American culture. Moses comments, "the child Claudia stands alone in her critique of a 'master' aesthetic that is internalized by nearly everyone in the community" including her own parents (Bloom. Ed. *Interpretations Updated* 131). Only when she is older will she conform to the prevailing racism of her society.

Frieda MacTeer is Claudia's ten-year-old sister. The two have a close relationship and tend to share the same opinions.

Rosemary Villanucci is a white girl who lives next door to the MacTeers despite the fact that her family is considerably richer. She sometimes tries to get Claudia and Frieda into trouble, and they sometimes beat her up, but otherwise they are friends.

Henry Washington is a bachelor who comes to the MacTeer house as a boarder, which is a considerable help with the family finances. Although he is seen as a serious and respectable man, he secretly has prostitutes over at the house, and one day he touches Frieda's breasts. Mr. MacTeer beats him up and throws him out.

The Breedlove Family and Associates

"The Breedlove's name … is bestowed with bitter irony; theirs is a self-hating family in which no love is bred" (Awkward, Bloom. Ed. *Interpretations* 89).

Cholly Breedlove is from Georgia. His marriage, which was once happy, has become a fairly constant physical battle between husband and wife. He is a heavy drinker given to violence. In the climax of the narrative, he rapes his only daughter, absconds when his crime is discovered, and eventually dies in the workhouse.

Pauline (Polly) Breedlove originally loved Cholly but has now taken refuge in considering herself a Christian martyr trapped in a marriage with a terrible sinner. She has a slightly deformed foot as the result of a childhood accident, but it is when she loses a front tooth that she begins to think of herself as ugly. Having totally bought into the absolute standard of white beauty, she finally realizes that it is not a standard that she can even imitate convincingly. Fick explains, "Try as she might, Pauline cannot be Jean Harlow, and the sense of inadequacy that comes from this failure is part of her tragedy" (Bloom. Ed. *Interpretations Updated* 25). The resulting sense of self-loathing she projects onto her own daughter whom she can no longer love. Increasingly Pauline finds happiness and meaning as housekeeper for the Fishers, an affluent white family, at the expense of neglecting her own home and children.

Sammy Breedlove is fourteen-years-old. He copes with his family's problems and his own unhappiness by repeatedly running away from home.

Pecola Breedlove is the ostensible protagonist of the novel. Eleven years old in 1941, she is the character most affected by the beauty standards of the dominant white culture. She sees herself as ugly and believes that having blue eyes will make her beautiful. Byerman notes, "Every scene in which she appears is used to show her lack of self-esteem and her passiveness … Whites, lighter-skinned blacks, and dark-skinned blacks who redirect their self-hatred, all make her feel her unworthiness" (Bloom Ed. *Interpretations* 5). She is raped by her father and becomes pregnant, but the baby is born prematurely and dies. Shortly afterwards, convinced that she has the blue eyes she coveted, she becomes insane, but not dangerously so and she continues to live with her mother.

Aunt Jimmy is the elderly woman who rescues Cholly from the rubbish tip on which his mother left him and brings him up.

Samson Fuller is, according to Aunt Jimmy, the father who abandoned Cholly's mother when she got pregnant. He lives in Macon, Georgia, but when Cholly finally tracks him down he wants nothing to do with Cholly.

Blue Jack is a co-worker of Cholly's during his teens. He is probably the closest thing to a father Cholly ever knows. A kind man and an excellent storyteller, drink finally gets the better of him.

M'Dear is an old woman who is a traditional healer in the community where Cholly grows up. She is called in to give her advice during Aunt Jimmy's final illness.

Darlene is the first girl with whom Cholly has sex. Two white hunters catch them in the act and insist that Cholly continues while they look on and laugh. Cholly's anger against the white men is misdirected towards Darlene. He never gets over the humiliation of this incident.

Other residents of Lorain, Ohio

Maureen Peal is a wealthy, light-skinned black girl who is very popular at school. She identifies herself with the white ideal of beauty and despises children who are darker in color.

Mr. Yacobowski is the local grocer. He is middle-aged and a white (presumably Jewish) immigrant who is uncomfortable with black customers.

China, Poland, and **Miss Marie** are three local prostitutes. In the eyes of the black community they are each "ruined" and decent people will have nothing to do with them. They stand as foils to those black women who aspire to white, middle class values because China, Poland, and Miss Marie are comfortable with their bodies (unattractive as they are). As a result, these women have no pretentiousness, feel no shame in their profession, and are quick to laugh and sing. They live above the Breedlove apartment and are the only people (except the MacTeers) who are always kind to Pecola. Miss Marie is known as the Maginot Line (a defensive military barrier on the eastern border of France) because of her considerable bulk.

Geraldine is typical of the middle-class black women from the South who have bought into the white value-system and have striven to eliminate every element of blackness from their personalities and their lives. Her house is immaculate, but she lacks passion for her husband, Louis, and love for her son, Junior. She feels real affection only for her cat.

Louis Junior is Geraldine's son. His mother has taught him to suppress every manifestation of his black being. Lacking genuine love from his mother, he becomes cruel and sadistic, projecting the humiliation that his black self has experienced onto anyone he senses to be weaker than himself. He harasses children who come to the nearby school playground which he considers his territory and tortures the family cat because he senses that it is the only thing that his mother cares for.

Soaphead Church is the latest generation of a light-skinned West Indian family which values its whiteness to such a degree that "they jeopardize their mental stability by intermarrying to maintain some semblance of whiteness" (Mbalia, Bloom Ed. *Interpretations* 156). Born Elihue Whitcomb, he added Micah meaning 'he who is like God.' After two months of marriage, his wife walked out on him, and he eventually moved to Lorain where he fraudulently advertises himself as a "Reader, Adviser, and Interpreter of Dreams." By 1941 he is an old man, but in his younger adulthood he satisfied his sexual appetite by seducing young girls (i.e., he is a pedophile).

Genres

Bildungsroman

The genre *Bildungsroman* (the term is of German origin) is a "novel of formation, novel of education, or coming-of-age story ... a literary genre that focuses on the psychological and moral growth of the protagonist from youth to adulthood, and in which, therefore, character change is extremely important" (Wikipedia article). Most novels of this genre end with the protagonist (normally male), wiser in the ways of the world and with greater self-knowledge, moving on to face the further challenges of adulthood.

It is true that Claudia, only nine at the time of the action, is younger than the protagonist in the normal *Bildungsroman*, but there is no doubt that by her friendship with Pecola in 1940-1, and the act of writing her narrative many years later, she achieves greater self-knowledge and a more profound understanding of what it means to be black in America in the second half of the twentieth century.

Feminist Fiction

Fairly obviously, *The Bluest Eye* has been seen as an example of feminist literature. The main characters of the novel are all women: although there is plenty of evidence of the corruption of black maleness in the novel, the focus is always on how black women are impacted by the loss of racial pride and community.

Claudia is in a literary tradition of assertive young women who defy the social and moral conventions of their age to achieve personal fulfillment. One may highlight Elizabeth Bennet (*Pride and Prejudice* by Jane Austen, 1813), the rebellious protagonist who marries Mr. Darcy for love and respect and not for money, and Jane Eyre (*Jane Eyre* by Charlotte Bronte, 1847) who overcomes every obstacle and prejudice to marry the blinded Mr. Rochester because she loves him passionately.

Historical Novel

The term historical fiction (or historical novel) applies to works set in a period at least twenty-five years before composition (e.g., a work such as Fenimore Cooper's *The Last of the Mohicans* which is set in 1757 and was written in 1826). On this criterion, Morrisons's book (published in 1970, thirty years after her narrative begins) just qualifies.

This raises the interesting question of why the author decided to set her story in America during World War II (though there are no explicit references to that conflict) and before the Civil Rights Movement of the 1960s. Partly, the answer may be that the novel is in some sense autobiographical: Claudia is the same age as Morrison was in 1940-1941, and she lives in Morrison's home town. A more fundamental reason is that the choice of period allows the author to show both the segregated South and the integrated North. Looking back on the history of the integration movement, it is tempting simply to assume that the end of segregation was a good thing for African Americans. However, some black activists stressed what was lost by integration: oral traditions and folktales, black communities, black schools and colleges, black music (the blues, which was increasingly appropriated by white musicians), black businesses – in a word, black identity. Morrison certainly has some sympathy with this view. *The Bluest Eye* celebrates the organic, supportive black communities of the South based on matriarchal extended families and chronicles their disintegration and the resulting vulnerability of black people to cultural racism.

Magical Realism

Magic, or magical, realism is a term first used in the 1955 essay "Magical Realism in Spanish American Fiction" by the critic Angel Floresto to describe narratives in which magical or supernatural events occur in an otherwise real-world setting and are described in the same matter-of-fact way. The novels of Gabriel García Márquez, particularly *One Hundred Years of Solitude*, are most often seen as exemplifying the genre.

The term is often used to describe Morrison's novels, particularly her later works. In *The Bluest Eye* there is magical thinking but the magic does not work – the sacrifice and the magic words that Claudia and Frieda use when planting the marigold seeds have no power to save the life of Pecola's unborn child, and neither Soaphead (a fraud in whose powers some believe) nor God actually turns Pecola's eyes blue. There are, however, two exceptions. The ancestor figure, M'Dear, appears virtually immortal, "Few could remember when M'Dear had not been around" (136). Her method of diagnosis involves a mystical communication with the disease through her hickory stick, and is shown to be accurate – Aunt Jimmy recovers her strength. Nature is a living force in the novel. There is certainly no rational explanation for the fact that not only did the sisters' marigolds not germinate, but "there were no marigolds in the fall of 1941" (5) because "the land of the entire country was hostile to marigolds that year" (206).

Narrative Voice

> Morrison tries to write novels that give the
> impression of having come from people who
> aren't writers. She wants it to appear as though
> no author tells the story. The narratives simply
> start and go on, apparently without a definite
> structure, unfolding and meandering in various
> directions all at once, it seems. (Carmean 11).

The novel is composed of a multiplicity of voices. A full list of the novel's
different voices is extensive: the children's reading primer; the first person
narrator, Claudia MacTeer; the impersonal third person omniscient narrator; the
first person narrative of Pauline Williams; the first person narrative of Soaphead
Church, the songs sung by various characters; the dialogue between Pecola and
her friend, which has no mediating narrator, and the final first person narrative
of the mature Claudia, which is significantly different from her other
contributions.

Claudia is the main first person narrator. Although her voice is that of the
mature Claudia who already knows the outcome of the story she tells, in every
chapter except the last she largely limits herself to relating her own life in 1941
and to reproducing her own naïve and frequently comically inaccurate
misunderstanding of events, with only occasional retrospective interpretive and
explanatory comments. What makes her a perceptive narrator is that at the age
of nine, as Gravett explains, "she has yet to accept the idea that she should be
forced to live by standards that will deny her own sense of self" (Bloom Ed.
Interpretations Updated 91). In the final chapter, however, the Claudia-narrator
makes full use of her adult perspective to provide a final interpretation of the
events that her eleven-year-old self observed. The reader understands that it is
only in telling the story that Claudia has come to see its full significance. The
narrator who wrote in her preface, "*There is nothing more to say – except why.
But* why *is difficult to handle, one must take refuge in* how" (6), is now ready to
explain *why*: the retelling of Pecola's story had enabled her to do so. The
obvious similarities between Claudia and the author have frequently been
noted: both grew up in Lorain, both were nine years old in 1941, and the girl
who wanted blue eyes is based on a school friend on Morrison's.

The third person omniscient narrator gives information about the
background of the characters that Claudia (even the mature Claudia) could not
possibly know and narrates contemporary incidents (such as Pecola's visit to
Soaphead Church) of which Claudia could have no direct knowledge.
Significantly, this narrator is non-judgmental. In providing the histories of the
three characters that play the key roles in the destruction of Pecola, her aim is to
explain not to justify or to condemn. The narrator does not attempt to defend

7

Cholly for what he does to Pecola, but she does show it as being too complicated for simple judgments, and leaves the reader in no doubt that, though Cholly is morally responsible for what happens to Pecola, he is also a victim.

Interspersed in the third person narrative of the chapters on Pauline Williams and Soaphead Church (though not that on Cholly Breedlove) are sections where we hear these characters' own voices. Pauline's stream of consciousness account of her relationship with Cholly speaks directly to the reader with the effect that it engages our sympathy. Soaphead's pedantic letter of self-justification to God does not engage our sympathy in the same way; rather it further alienates the reader from him. One other significant voice in the narrative is that of song, always black song whether it be gospel or blues. Song has the ability to strengthen; each song is an act of resistance. As Wong writes, "the blues provide a means to gather and to transmute the pain of daily existence" (Bloom Ed. *Interpretations* 149).

In the final chapter, there is a dialogue between Pecola and her friend which has no narrator (either first or third person) to place it in context. The reader is required to make sense of it without a mediating voice. Interestingly, the third person omniscient narrator does not reappear in this chapter. It is the voice of the mature Claudia which ends the novel and it is her character, writing from within the narrative, that provides a subjective judgment on the significance of Pecola's fate. Dittmar perceptively comments that Morrison's "use of a multi-voiced community" in her narrative "acknowledges the insufficiency of any one voice. It posits, rather, that knowledge is constructed by the many and that reading is a process of active reshaping by readers" (Bloom. Ed. *Interpretations* 127-128). This explains the non-appearance of the third person omniscient narrator in the final chapter. The reader is given Claudia's assessment of why things happened as they did: it is a viewpoint that the reader respects, but it is a subjective viewpoint and therefore not the novel's final meaning which remains in the mind of the reader.

Mbalia's essay "The Need for Racial Approbation" argues that the narrative diversity of the novel is a fundamental weakness. (See Bloom Ed. *Interpretations* 153-161.) This is a viewpoint with which Morrison herself has agreed. She has written that her use of both a first and a third person narrator "made a 'shambles' of her text: 'I resorted to two voices, [...] both of which are extremely unsatisfactory to me'" (quoted by Malmgren, Bloom. Ed. *Interpretations Updated* 147).

Setting

The setting of the action is Lorain, Ohio, but several of the main characters have been born and brought up in the Old South having been part of the northward migration of black people in the first half of the twentieth century in search of jobs and a better life. Thus, Pauline William's childhood is spent in Alabama before her family moves to Kentucky, "where there were mines and mill-work" (111), and Geraldine is typical of the educated, upwardly mobile young black women who have come to Ohio from "Meridian, Mobile, Aiken, and Baton Rouge" (81). After Pauline marries Colly, himself "a Georgia black boy" (152), the two "go way up north, where Colly said steel mills were begging for workers" (116).

The contrast between the rural South and the urban North is fundamental to the novel. In leaving the South, the black characters improve their lives materially but impoverish them emotionally for they lose touch with their black roots. The pervasive racism of Lorain may be less overt and less violent than the racism that blacks have suffered in Alabama or Georgia, but it is more debilitating because there is no unified black community to offer counter-values based in the West African culture from which these people came. Pauline explains the difference she immediately perceived between Alabama and Ohio:

> *I weren't used to so much white folks. The ones*
> *I seed before was something hateful, but they*
> *didn't come around too much ... Northern*
> *colored folks were different too ... No better*
> *than whites for meanness. They could make*
> *you feel no-count, 'cept I didn't expect it from*
> *them.* (117)

What is lacking in Ohio is the organic black culture that still survives in the South (as seen in the community's response to Aunt Jilly's sickness and in the aftermath of her death) for the black population of Lorain has bought into the value system of the oppressive whites. The matriarchal extended family of the South has been replaced by the patriarchal nuclear family of the North. As a result, as Thomas explains:

> Lorain ... is a world of grotesques –
> individuals whose psyches have been
> deformed by their efforts to assume false
> identities, their failures to achieve meaningful
> identities, or simply their inability to retain and
> communicate love. (Bloom Ed. *Interpretations*
> 226-227)

In Lorain, Cholly is less likely to find himself looking down the barrel of a white hunter's gun, but Pauline will find no support network of proud black women which could form a counterbalance to the pervasive societal racism that black characters experience every day at the store, in the movies, on the billboards, when they eat a Mary Jane candy, or when they drink from a Shirley Temple cup. That is why when Cholly burns down their house, the Breedloves have to rely on the state to step in with support. They have no network of kin and friends to support them through their time of trial.

Themes

The title, *The Bluest Eye*, reflects Pecola's longing to have the bluest eyes in the world which will make her pretty and so make others value her. It is also a play on the words 'melancholy me' (blue being the color associated with melancholy and 'eye' being a homonym for the pronoun 'I') which also describe Pecola. Finally blue suggests 'the blues' a doleful kind of black music, and in this sense the 'I' is Claudia whose blues song the novel is.

Racism

After an exchange between Cholly and a ticket clerk at a bus station in which the clerk calls him a '"lying nigger"' (ironically, the clerk is actually quite sympathetic and lets Cholly pay the child rate for his ticket), the narrator explains that such insults "were part of the nuisances of life, like lice" (153). Similarly, when the store owner Mr. Yacobowski "does not see her [Pecola], because for him there is nothing to see" (48), the narrator explains that "this vacuum was not new to her … [Pecola] has seen it lurking in the eyes of all white people" (49). Fundamentally, then, the experience of black people is the same whether they live in the South or the North. There are, however, important differences. In his teens, Cholly's friend Blue tells him "how he talked his way out of getting lynched once, and how others hadn't" (134), and Cholly has his own encounter with armed white hunters. In Ohio, however, black people encounter a form of cultural racism which, though less physically dangerous, erodes their confidence in their own being. It is this that interests Morrison – the continuing racism of the post-Civil Rights, post-integration period.

The Bluest Eye is set in 1941, thirteen years before the United States Supreme Court ruled in Brown v. Board of Education of Topeka (1954) that state laws mandating separate public schools for black and white students were unconstitutional. Nevertheless, Claudia, Frieda and Pecola attend an integrated school (albeit one in which the black students separate themselves from the white and vice versa), and the MacTeer family house (which is presumably typical of other black characters) is in an integrated neighborhood. What has been lost, however, is the mutually supportive black communities and extended families which segregation in the South actually encouraged; they have been replaced by an emphasis on the nuclear family and individualism.

Central to the novel is, as Peach explains:

> the distortion of the self created by the imposition of white norms on black people. The effect of this imposition is to create a profound sense of fracture. The concept of black in the novel is a construct partly of the characters' own making but mostly social based on white definitions of blackness which

associate it with violence, poverty, dirt and lack of education, whilst Africa is perceived as uncivilized and (negatively) tribal. (Bloom Ed. *Interpretations* 172)

Morrison explores the traumatic experience of social powerlessness and of devalued racial identity. This is most obviously evident in the educated and ambitious Southern black women who "wash themselves with orange-colored Lifebuoy soap, dust themselves with Cashmere Bouquet talc, clean their teeth with salt on a piece of rag, soften their skin with Jergens Lotion ... straighten their hair with Dixie Peach..." (82). In the men, it is shown through the hard work that they have to perform in insecure manual jobs just to keep their families financially afloat. By aspiring to become white, black people are inevitably setting themselves up for failure which they erroneously blame on their own imperfections. In the case of both men and women, the resulting self-hatred is frequently projected onto others with various degrees of viciousness. The ultimate act of projection is Cholly's forced intercourse with Darlene which the narrator describes thus, "With a violence born of total helplessness, he pulled her dress up, lowered his trousers and underwear... He hated her. He almost wished he could do it – hard, long, and painfully, he hated her so much" (148).

At the same time, the novel suggests the qualities that might permit strong black people to survive. These qualities are evident in the black communities in the South, but up in Ohio they exist only precariously in individuals. Of these, the most important is nine-year-old Claudia (since Frieda remains a rather shadowy figure) who consciously stands out against, and in her narrative denounces, the universal message that 'White is Beautiful.' Nowhere does Claudia articulate her passionate belief in the beauty of blackness than in her visualization of Pecola's baby:

> It was in a dark, wet place, its head covered with great O's of wool, the black face holding, like nickels, two clean black eyes, the flared nose, kissing-thick lips, and the living breathing silk of black skin ... More strongly than my fondness for Pecola, I felt a need for someone to want the black baby to live – just to counteract the universal love of white baby dolls, Shirley Temples, and Maureen Peels. (190)

Yet even Claudia admits that, as she grew older, she too succumbed to the universal adoration of the Shirley Temple paradigm of female beauty, as if racial self-loathing were a necessary part of maturation. In the novel, the post-integration African American community of Ohio has no unifying racial culture and fails to understand the true nature of the economic forces that are keeping them down.

The White Standard of Beauty

Morrison places the emphasis on examining the cultural values that rob black females of their pride in being who they are. Given that the main characters (Pecola, Claudia and Frieda) are just entering or about to enter puberty, the focus falls even more precisely on the coming of age of black girls in desegregated America in the early 1940s. As we have seen, black women are particularly vulnerable to the white ideal of beauty that pervades all aspects of culture. Carmean comments that "The pervasive *white* standard of beauty adopted by so many characters in *The Bluest Eye* is at the heart of the cruelty and destruction that occurs because it fails to recognize and value difference" (20). That standard is evident in the white baby dolls given to Claudia and in the idealization of Shirley Temple and other adult white movie stars. In the daily lives of the characters, the internalized of this absolute standard is evident in the popularity of light-skinned Maureen and in Mrs. Breedlove's preference for the little white girl, for whose family (the Fishers) she works, over her own daughter.

In describing Claudia's reaction to the white dolls she is given as presents, Morrison was quite aware that she was constructing an atypical character. In May 1951, Dr. Kenneth B. Clark conducted a series of tests to study black children's attitudes about race using white and brown dolls. Sixteen black children participated: ten preferred the white doll; eleven used the word 'bad' to describe the brown doll; nine used the word 'nice' to describe the white doll; and seven chose the white doll when asked which doll was most like themselves. Clark reported that one of the children expressed a preference for the white doll because, "it's got blue eyes – 'cause it's got pretty eyes." Morrison is consciously referencing this research in the novel. (See Douglas, Bloom Ed. *Interpretations Updated* 216-218.)

Awkward explains that "The black characters of *The Bluest Eye* appear to accept Western standards of beauty, morality, and success despite (for the most part) being unable themselves to achieve these standards" (Bloom Ed. *Interpretations* 72). Adult black men and women have learned to hate their own blackness and the effect is that they hate their own bodies: the men take their hatred out on their wives, and the wives take their hatred out on their children. Pecola is the ultimate victim of this projection: her mother, despite her resolution to love her daughter, sees her as ugly, and the lighter-skinned Geraldine curses Pecola's blackness. Pecola connects beauty with being loved and "faced with the pervasiveness of Western cultural standards of beauty, accepts unquestioningly the myth's validity" (Awkward, Bloom. Ed. *Interpretations* 76). She believes that if she possesses blue eyes, the cruelty in her life will be replaced by affection and respect. This hopeless desire leads ultimately to madness.

With the exception of Claudia, only occasional rebellions occur, as in the case of "'that crazy old nigger'" who married and then deserted Miss Della Jones, that good church woman who always kept her house and her person clean and perfumed, because "'he wanted a woman to smell like a woman. Said Della was too clean for him'" (13) or in the case of the three whores. Such voices (they are few) announce that 'Black is Beautiful.'

Seeing Oneself and Being Seen by Others

Carmean writes that "If one takes all her writing into account ... it seems apparent that even though she does not specify it as such, [Morrison's] grand theme is actually that of self-discovery, or its close variation, the issue of self-definition" (15). The problem that most characters in the novel face is that American culture has taught them to undervalue and despise what they actually are. Yet they are unable, or unwilling, to see the true nature of their powerlessness which resides in historical, cultural, economic and psychological factors over which they have no control. Instead, they blame themselves (they blame their blackness) and each other because to become aware would precipitate a rage that would be self-destructive since they know themselves to be impotent to fight institutionalized racism. Claudia is the only character who is able to articulate her anger at being seen unfairly because of her race. She alone acknowledges her own anger and feels justified in feeling it, but eventually (as she admits early in her narrative) she too lost her anger, which is why in the final chapter she blames the black community of Lorain for what happened to Pecola rather than the white racism which is really to blame.

Claudia writes of herself and Frieda, "Guileless and without vanity, we were still in love with ourselves then" (74). Completely lacking Claudia's sense of pride in her black self, Pecola believes that the cruelty she experiences is a result of the fact that others see her as ugly, when, of course, it is the result of the fact that she sees herself as ugly when she is beautiful. Pecola takes refuge in fantasy and magical thinking. If she had beautiful blue eyes, she believes, people would not do ugly things in front of her or to her, "It had occurred to Pecola some time ago that if her eyes, those eyes that held the pictures, and knew the sights—if those eyes of hers were different, that is to say, beautiful, she herself would be different" (46). Following her visit to Soaphead, she is finally able to see herself as beautiful, but only at the cost of her losing her ability to function in the world around her.

Sexual Abuse

The novel is not one story told from a single perspective: what happened to Pecola is told by multiple voices whose personal narratives each provide a partial account. The crime of which Cholly is guilty is one of the most heinous imaginable (recall that we are also told that he killed three white men before he met Pauline), but Morrison sets out in the novel to understand how it happened without in any way excusing or condoning it. The same may be said of the pedophilia of Mr. Henry Washington and Soaphead Church, for each there are reasons (sometimes reasons going back generations), though there is no suggestion that these reasons absolve the men of moral, and legal, responsibility.

Black women in the novel are doubly powerless, "White women said, 'Do this.' White children said, 'Give me that.' White men said, 'Come here.' Black men said, 'Lay down'" (138). Like the males, they have lost control of their bodies since they are ordered about by whites, but they are also at the mercy of black men when it comes to sex. For obvious reason, black women are at their most vulnerable when they are young like the victims of Mr. Henry, Soaphead and Cholly. Sexual coming-of-age in an environment where men assume that they have the right to abuse young girls is full of danger. What makes young girls more vulnerable is their lack of knowledge about sex. When Pecola menstruates for the first time, she asks if she is going to die; when Frieda hears that she might have been "ruined" by Mr. Henry's touching, she is convinced that she is going to get fat. Neither Mrs. MacTeer (who is a loving mother) nor Mrs. Breedlove (who is not) has prepared their daughters for the onset of puberty.

Healthy Sexual Appetites

Against this rather somber picture of sexual abuse, the novel does celebrate healthy sexuality. This is most obvious in Pauline's lyrical descriptions of her love making with Cholly in their years of happiness together. She describes her experience of orgasm as feeling "rainbow all inside" (131). Another example is Cholly's first sexual experience with Darlene, before it is perverted and sullied by the two white racists (145-147). What is significant is that the sex is tender and consensual (in fact, it is Darlene who initiates the intimate touching). Finally, one might add the guiltless pleasure that the three whores obviously have in sex.

The novel suggests that sexual desire should be a source of pleasure and that the denial of the body results from self-hatred and shame. Willis explains that "Claudia ... is fascinated by all bodily functions and the physical residues of living in the world. She rebels at being washed, finding her scrubbed body obscene due to its "dreadful and humiliating absence of dirt" (Bloom. Ed. *Interpretations* 49). In contrast, Geraldine is one of those black women who, aspiring to live by white standards, is disgusted by the messiness of sex, "She hopes he will not sweat – the damp may get into her hair; and that she will remain dry between her legs – she hates the glucking sound they make when she is moist" (84). As a result, she fakes her orgasms and has sex as little as possible. The inability of black characters (both male and female) to enjoy the pleasures of their own bodies is not the least significant of the effects of generations of racism.

Symbols

Flight

As Awkward points out:

> Pecola's tragic plight ... stems primarily from
> her inability to achieve a positive reading of
> blackness in an urban setting dominated by
> pervasive white standards ... This pervasive
> whiteness, coupled with her victimization at
> the hands of self-protective African-Americans
> who view her as the shadow of blackness
> causes her almost literally to transform into ...
> a grotesque, flightless bird" (Bloom. Ed.
> *Interpretations* 100).

It is worth pausing to trace the bird imagery associated with Pecola. The first indication of her fatally damaged psyche follows the incident where Pecola's blackness is savaged after school by the gang of black boys and then by the light-skinned high-yellow Maureen. Claudia describes how Pecola "seemed to fold into herself, like a pleated wing" (73). However, the damage done to Pecola's psyche by being raped takes away the possibility of flight. Describing Pecola "walking up and down" following her nervous collapse, Claudia says, "Elbows bent, hands, on shoulders, she flailed her arms like a bird in an eternal, grotesque futile effort to fly. Beating the air, a winged but grounded bird, intent on the blue void it could not reach – could not even see – but which filled the valleys of her mind" (204).

Communion

The ultimate embodiment of the white ideal of beauty is the Virgin Mary. Mr. Yacobowski, the store owner, does not see Pecola because his mind has been "honed on the doe-eyed Virgin Mary," and he "senses that he need not waste the effort of a glance ... [at] a little black girl" (48). Thus, when Pecola drinks milk (three quarts!) from the rather tacky Shirley Temple cup, it becomes a symbolic chalice, and she is taking communion, ingesting "the blood of the goddess in order to become her" (Gibson, Bloom. Ed. *Interpretations* 110). Similarly, when Pecola buys and eats the three, one penny packets of Mary Janes (there are three candies in each packet), she is symbolically eating the communion wafer (the body of Christ), "To eat the candy is somehow to eat the eyes, eat Mary Jane. Love Mary Jane. Be Mary Jane" (50). Gibson writes, "Transubstantiation has occurred; the candy has been transformed into the body and blood of Mary Jane," and, we may add, of Shirley Temple, all of the white film actresses mentioned, and Jane who appears in the primer (Op. cit. 111). The narrator describes the religious ecstasy that Pecola experiences as "nine lovely orgasms with Mary Jane" (50).

Nature

The importance of nature in the novel can hardly be doubted. The four sections into which the narrative is divided are named for the seasons beginning in the autumn of 1940 and concluding in the autumn of 1941 with the failure of the Marigolds to germinate. Given the urban setting of the story, the closeness of humans to nature is perhaps surprising.

The precise significance of nature symbolism in the novel is a matter for dispute among critics. What we can say is that, in the childhood memories of Claudia, each season is a time of trial: winter is bitterly cold, a time of no gardens, of sickness, and of false spring days; spring is a time of flexible branches which means that it is "shot through with the remembered ache of switchings" (97); summer is a time of "dust and lowering skies ... a season of storms" (187); and autumn is, of course, a time of the failure of germination, both vegetable and human, when seeds dropped into "our little plot of black earth" (6) fail because the very earth itself is "unproductive" (5). Dittmar accurately concludes that "Morrison's four-part design implies a trap" (Bloom Ed. *Interpretations* 128). Mbalia identifies that trap arguing convincingly that "the infertile soil of Lorain, Ohio, symbolic of the United States, precludes the healthy, normal growth of the marigolds, symbolic of African-American people" (Bloom Ed. *Interpretations* 158).

The result of the nature symbolism is certainly a despairing novel, but that despair does not seem to be universal or elemental. It is related to the migration of the black characters in this novel from the South in search of employment in the industrialized northern states, which is a movement away from an organic black community to pseudo-white respectability. Pauline unconsciously highlights this loss when she notes that leaving Alabama was "the last time I seen real june bugs. These things up here ain't june bugs. They's something else" (112), and consciously when she tells the reader that for her everything changed once she and Cholly moved to Lorain, "It was hard to get to know folks up here ... I weren't used to so much white folks ... Northern colored folk was different too ... No better than whites for meanness" (117). Thus the symbolism of nature as an antagonist is related to what Willis calls "[t]he problem at the center of Morrison's writing" which is to examine how black people can "maintain an Afro-American cultural heritage once the relationship to the black rural South has been stretched over distance and generations" (Bloom Ed. *Interpretations* 47). The "earth" that is "unyielding" is the land that America has become (5).

Houses and Homes

The first sentence of the novel, from a Dick-and-Jane child's reader, establishes the house as a symbol: "Here is the house" (1). In the novel, there are, of course, the houseless characters, like the "'old crazy nigger'" who walks out on his wife, Miss Della, and Mr. Henry Washington, who is a perennial boarder, like Soaphead Church. To Claudia, being homeless, or "outdoors," is "the real terror of life" since it means having nowhere to go (17). All of the families portrayed in the novel are nuclear families, so the house in which members live indicates both a family's economic and emotional security. In terms of economics, the most expensive and beautiful house belongs to Geraldine; the MacTeer house is old and drafty; and the store front inhabited by the Breedloves is hardly a house at all. In terms of emotion, however, the MacTeer house is a home in which the sisters feel cared for, loved and protected, despite the shortcomings of their parents; Geraldine's house is a place where feelings are repressed and love neither given not sought; and the Breedlove house is a place of discord and violence.

Study Guide: Questions and Commentary

The questions are designed to be used on your first reading of the story (though they can, of course, be used if you happen to have read the story already). The aim is not to test you but to help you to understand the text. The questions do not normally have simple answers, nor is there always one answer. Consider a range of possible interpretations – preferably by discussing the questions with others. Disagreement is encouraged!

For the reasons stated above, no answers are provided, though you will find that the commentary sections cover most of the issues raised in the questions.

"Here is the house..."

Questions

1. In what kind of book would you normally expect a text like this to be? How would the text look different in such a book?

2. The text is printed three times. What exactly are the differences between the three versions? What do you think is the significance of these differences?

Commentary

The opening paragraph appears to be the beginning of the text of a children's reader. The sentences have a few simple structures that are repeated, almost all of the words are monosyllables, and key words are also repeated. All of this is designed to make the text easy to read. The family (Mother, Father, Dick, and Jane) appear to live an idyllic, suburban life: they have a "pretty" house and are "very happy" as a family. The Dick and Jane readers, by William Elson and William Gray, were in use in American elementary schools from the 1930s through to the 1970s. The series has been criticized because it treats "American childhood as an abstraction that excludes all but white middle class children" (Werrlein, Bloom Ed. *Interpretations Updated* 197). The text is not taken from an actual Dick and Jane reader.

Although nothing at all is said about the race of the characters, their names make it quite clear that they are white. Early readers usually have lots of pictures in which members of the family would be shown as white. As Gibson points out, "the act of learning to read and write means exposure to the values of the culture from which the reading material emanates ... One cannot simply learn to read without being subjected to the values engraved in the text" (Bloom. Ed. *Interpretations* 107). Morrison herself has commented that "The primer with white children was the way life was presented to black people." That life involved a nuclear family in which the father was the bread-winner and the mother the homemaker.

There are, however, undertones in the description of the 'ideal' family that the reader should not miss. The absence of the pictures that would accompany this text in a child's primer makes the reader aware of how abrupt and discontinuous the sentences are. The narrative focuses on Jane who wants to play, but can find no one to play with her: the kitten will not play; Jane's mother laughs; her father smiles; and the dog runs away. Strangely, Dick is not even asked to play; he is effectively absent from the text. No one responds directly to Jane's evident desire for a playmate, leaving Jane completely isolated. Although the text does not say anything about the emotions of its characters, it is all rather sad, ironically undercutting the positivity of the way Jane's life as a family member is described. The disconnected sentences of the text mirror the lack of emotional connection between Jane and the members of her "happy" family: the contentment that the passage celebrates is an appearance only. Then a friend comes to play with Jane and she is no longer alone (as Pecola will no longer be alone at the end of the narrative).

The primer text is repeated twice, the first time without punctuation and the second time without either punctuation or word spaces. It progressively disintegrates before our eyes, becoming a meaningless conglomeration of letters. Klotman has suggested that the first version represents the idealized white family; the second version represents the MacTeer family, in which the parents are loving and caring but poor and not always emotionally supportive of their children; and the third version represents the dysfunctional Breedlove family, in which the parents have neither love not money (Awkward, Bloom. Ed. *Interpretations* 68). Other critics argue that the progressive disintegration of meaning is the textual equivalent of Claudia's dismemberment of her white dolls so that the third version comes to symbolize the essentially self-destructive nature of the values inherent in the original text. Since the two interpretations are not mutually exclusive, the reader does not have to choose between them.

The contrast between the idealized, white upper-middle-class family of Dick and Jane and the imperfect Breedlove family described in the narrative is emphasized by the use of excerpts from the primer used as chapter headings when the voice of the text is the third person omniscient narrator. As Werrlein explains, "Just as the Dick and Jane stories equate white privilege with a historyless version of white Americanness, the poverty and suffering of Morrison's Breedlove family symbolizes America's brutal history of racial persecution in the United States" (Bloom Ed. *Interpretations Updated* 198).

"Quiet as it's kept…"

Questions

3. Explain why it was so important to the two sisters that their marigolds should germinate in the fall of 1941.

Commentary

The bland, timeless, impersonal third person narrative of the previous extract is replaced by the voice of an unnamed first person narrator who is looking back to the fall of 1941 when she and her sister were children. True, the sex of the narrator is not explicitly stated, but her close relationship with her sister and her concern for the birth of a baby strongly imply a female perspective.

Two shocking facts about the fall of 1941 are juxtaposed: the many marigold seeds that the narrator and her sister planted did not sprout, and neither did any other marigolds in the community; and the baby that Pecola was having (her father's baby) died. Evidently these two facts are related in the mind of the narrator who is still troubled by them. In some magical way, the girls believed that if they could make their seeds grow then Pecola's baby would survive. Their failure resulted in the loss of the sisters' *"innocence and faith."* A sense of guilt pervades the account. The adult narrator feels the need to explain *why* the *"seeds shriveled and died; her baby too,"* but because causation is *"difficult to handle,"* she will *"take refuge in* how" (6).

Certain conclusions are drawn immediately. The narrator tells us that her sister was wrong – the marigolds did not fail to germinate because the narrator had planted the seeds too deeply. Neither was the failure due the fact that Pecola was pregnant with her own father's child. The sisters' *"magic,"* by which they tried to ensure the *"health and safe delivery of Pecola's baby,"* simply did not work. The disturbing truth is that the very earth was *"unyielding"* – it would not allow life either to the marigold seeds or to the seed that Pecola's father had implanted. What happened was, in the truest sense of the word, a tragedy: Pecola's baby died and with it the sisters' innocence. Pecola's father is now dead, and only Pecola and the earth remain.

A Comparison

Questions

4. What are the main differences between the stories told in the two prologues and the manner in which they are told?

Commentary

The two texts are very different. The first presents a disjointed succession of incidents with no explicit narrative connection except that they are all related to the storybook Jane. The action is played out by stereotypical characters that appear to have no emotional connection with one another. The second is a complex, personal narrative in which the links between characters and incidents are explored by an adult narrator still struggling to understand them. The characters are connected emotionally, though that connection ranges from love and caring to sexual abuse. Thus, Cholly Breedlove (the irony of the name is immediately obvious) has had an incestuous relationship with his daughter, and the sisters are concerned for both Pecola, who is their friend, and for her baby. There is a lingering sense of guilt that their "magic" failed to ensure the birth of either the marigolds or the baby.

Autumn

"Nuns go by..."

Questions

5. In what ways is the house in which Claudia lives different from Dick and Jane's house?

6. In what ways is Claudia's mother different from Jane's mother?

7. What exactly does it mean for a family to be "outdoors"? Why is the possibility of this happening a constant fear among members of the black community?

Commentary

The first chapter has the same narrator as the previous section: she is Claudia MacTeer and she had an older sister Frieda. At the time covered by the narrative, they are nine and ten respectively. In some ways, Claudia's life is pretty good: she has a father, a mother and a sister, and they lived in a large house. However, the house in which the MacTeers live is very different from Jane's "very pretty" house. The latter is colorful, "It is green and white. It has a red door" (5), while Claudia's house is "old, cold, and green." The ill-fitting windows have to be stuffed with rags to keep out the drafts, and only one room is lighted at night, the others being "braced in darkness, peopled by roaches and mice" (10). Even sleeping in bed is a constant battle with the cold in winter.

Claudia looks back on her childhood and, of course, understands things that were confusing to her when she was nine. To her and Frieda, adults in general are unpredictable and children have a hard time understanding them, "Adults do not talk to us – they give us directions. They issue orders without providing information" (10). Mrs. MacTeer has a volatile temper and tends to react both verbally and physically in ways that her children find deeply hurtful. When Pecola drinks three quarts of milk, Mrs. MacTeer goes into one of her "fussing soliloquies" which can last for hours when, "having told everybody and everything off, she would burst into song..." (24). Later, their white friend Rosaline reports that Claudia and Frieda are "'playing nasty'" (30). Their mother believes the accusation and, despite the girls' pleas of innocence, begins to slap Frieda on the legs. The narrator recalls, "Frieda was destroyed. Whippings wounded and insulted her" (31). Only when Mrs. MacTeer has blown off steam, or in the case of the whipping discovered what the girls were really doing, does she return to her cheerful and loving self, "she pulled both of them [Frieda and Pecola] toward her, their heads against her stomach. Her eyes were sorry" (31). When Claudia catches a cold her mother is angry and only with the perspective of hindsight does Claudia understand "that she is not angry at me but at my sickness" (11). Unlike Jane, whose mother seems indifferent to her, Mrs. MacTeer does everything she can to nurse her sick daughter back to health. In retrospect, Claudia admits that even as a child she knew that she was loved. She tells us, "Love, thick and dark as Agala syrup, eased up into that cracked window … When I think of autumn, I think of somebody with hands who does not want me to die" (12). Jane's mother won't even play with her!

Another insecurity that plagues Claudia is her consciousness that her family is poor (despite a hard-working father), clinging to security and respectability, with the ever-present threat of homelessness. Her house is in need of repairs that the parents do not have the money to do, and she and Frieda go along in the evening with adults to "fill burlap sacks with the tiny pieces of coal lying about" along the railway tracks (10). The very first incident shows the sisters looking at their "next-door friend" Rosemary Villanucci, who is white, taunting them from inside her father's Buick where she is eating bread and butter." The MacTeers have no car, and to supplement the family income the mother takes in a boarder, Mr. Henry Washington, whose "'Five dollars every two weeks'" will be a great help to the family finances (15).

Poverty and homelessness is an ever-present threat to members of the black community. Pecola is an object of pity to the sisters because they are aware that her father has put the family "outdoors" which Claudia calls "the real terror of life." It is this terror that leads black people to repress "[e]very possibility of excess" (17) and to strive to own their own property, for ownership offers security. In this they are buying into the American Dream that through hard work everyone can buy themselves "'some nice little old place'" (18). The reality, however, is that the blacks in Lorain are "a minority in both caste and class … on the hem of life, struggling to consolidate our weakness and hang on…" (17). As Kuenz points out, "The result is a community of individuals who are, at times, painfully alienated from each other as each is divided within him- or herself" (Bloom Ed. *Interpretations Updated* 108).

The gossip between Mrs. MacTeer and her friends about the various scandals in the neighborhood (the "'crazy old nigger'" who left Miss Della with "'[o]ne of Old Slack Bessie's girls'"; Hattie who "'wasn't never right'" in the head; and Auntie Julia, apparently senile, who "'is still trotting up and down Sixteenth Street talking to herself'" [13]) clearly indicates the failure of the community to support its weaker individuals, and in doing so it foreshadows Claudia's final verdict that the community failed Pecola (see 204-206).

The most insidious effect of white racism, however, is that it presents black women with an ideal of physical beauty which they can never attain. This ideal is exemplified by the Hollywood stars of the day such as Betty Grable, Jean Harlow and (especially) the child-star Shirley Temple. When Mr. Henry introduces himself to Claudia and Frieda he says, "Hello there. You must be Greta Garbo, and you must be Ginger Rogers" (16). He means it as a witty complement, and it is received as such, but as Kuenz points out he is effectively "reducing [the sisters] to type in a kind of objectification which, in part, will make it easier for him later to molest Frieda" (*Op. cit.* 104). It is Pecola, however, who is most invested in the white ideal of feminine beauty. She loves drinking out of the Shirley Temple cup, and "took every opportunity to drink milk out of it just to handle and see sweet Shirley's face" (23). Her obsession leads her to drink three quarts of milk! In contrast, Claudia feels "unsullied hatred" for Shirley Temple (19) and for the children's dolls that she is given which are always white and blue-eyed. These Claudia gets as Christmas gifts because "nobody ever asked me what I wanted for Christmas" (being uninterested in motherhood she did not want *any kind* of doll), and because the adults have bought into the white definition of beauty. Claudia cannot understand the beauty that others see in these dolls. She recalls:

> I had only one desire: to dismember it. To see
> of what it was made, to discover the dearness,
> to find the beauty, the desirability that has
> escaped me, but apparently only me. (20)

In this way, Claudia destroys every doll she is ever given without discovering the secret of white beauty. Having failed to locate an answer, Claudia transfers the same destructive impulse to little white girls who she also wants to dismember in order to discover the elusive "secret of the magic they weaved on others" (22). As an adult, she informs the reader, she "learned how repulsive this disinterested violence was" and became ashamed of it.

Throughout the chapter, whiteness is associated with cleanliness – as though, by washing, black people might become white. This is why black adults "fussed and fidgeted over their hard-won homes" (18); why black adults curtail any impulse toward luxuries; why Claudia must have a "hateful bath in a galvanized zinc tub" in order to put on a new dress for a tea party (22). Unthinkingly, the black community seeks to live by white standards. Yet there are rebels. There is the "'crazy old nigger'" who leaves Miss Della because, as he said, "'he wanted a woman to smell like a woman. Said Della was too clean for him'" (13). Then there is the rebellious Claudia who bemoans "the dreadful and humiliating absence of dirt" when her mother has forced her to take a bath. To Claudia, the ink and other marks on her body are evidence of how she has spent the day, in contrast with which cleanliness is "irritable, unimaginative" (22). Ironically, the narrator admits that she eventually grew out of her rebellious phase and learned to "worship" Shirley Temple and "to delight in cleanliness," yet she admits that, even as she learned these values, she was aware "that the change was adjustment without improvement" (23).

Given the ages of the three girls, the topic of sex is important to them all: it is an exciting and frightening mystery. The unmarried Mr. Henry Washington, who has the reputation of being a steady worker with quiet ways (and who comes to the MacTeer house washed and smelling "wonderful" [15]), has girlie magazines hidden in his room, and there is ominous foreshadowing in his trick with the penny that has Frieda and Claudia searching him all over for the vanished penny. But the most significant sexual event is when Pecola begins to menstruate and therefore, Frieda informs her, becomes physically able to conceive. There is a particular poignancy in her question, "'How do you do that? I mean, how do you get somebody to love you?'" For Pecola the answer to that question will be tied up with the white ideal of beauty.

"HEREISTHEHOUSEITISGREENANDWHITE..."

Questions

8. Create a timeline showing the occupancy and businesses of the house in which the Breedloves briefly live around 1941.

9. In what specific ways is life in the Breedlove house inferior to life in the MacTeer house?

Commentary

This chapter is immediately different from the others that have gone before. The margins are justified both left and right, and the narrator is an anonymous third person. The title of the chapter is from the description of the pretty house in the Dick and Jane children's story. As Hedin explains, "The seven central elements of Jane's world – house, cat, Mother [*sic*], father, dog, and friend – become, in turn, plot elements, but only after they are inverted to fit the realities of Pecola's world" (Awkward, Bloom Ed. *Interpretations* 68). By contrast, the chapter itself describes the rundown apartment, formerly a store front, where the Breedloves live after Cholly Breedlove comes out of jail. If the MacTeer home falls short of the pretty house, the Breedlove house is its antithesis. It is "a box of peeling gray" (34) in which "joylessness stank, pervading everything" (36). The old furniture, which shows no evidence of human contact, has been "conceived, manufactured, shipped, and sold in various states of thoughtlessness, greed, and indifference" (35). None of the furniture holds pleasant memories for the humans who live there. This is epitomized by the couch which, though purchased new, was delivered with a split down the middle, and the store refused to take it back. The store would never have done this had the buyer been white, so the couch becomes a symbol of the economic powerlessness of the Breedlove family. Similarly, the coal stove is unpredictable, but the fire is always dead in the morning.

If the members of Jane's "happy" family seem, on reflection, emotionally unattached, the third person omniscient narrator explicitly states that each member of the Breedlove family lives "in his own cell of consciousness, each making his own patchwork quilt of reality ... [from] fragments of experience here, pieces of information there." Effectively, there *is* no family, though each person "created a sense of belonging and tried to make do with the way they found each other" (34).

The continuing ugliness of the abandoned storefront and its refusal, in subsequent years, to blend in with the surrounding buildings symbolizes the ugliness of the Breedloves' story.

"HERE IS THE FAMILY MOTHER…"

Questions

10. In what sense(s) are the Breedloves ugly, and in what sense(s) are they not ugly?

11. Why does Cholly need the fights with his wife? Why does Mrs. Breedlove need her husband to get drunk and behave badly?

12. Pecola engages in magical thinking about solutions to her misery. Give examples.

13. What is so hurtful about the way Mr. Yacobowski treats Pecola? How does she react?

14. What does the account of Pecola's visit to the three whores add to the reader's understanding of the basic themes of the novel?

Commentary

The title is a description of the family that lives in the pretty house in the Dick and Jane story. In stark contrast, the chapter describes the tempestuous relationship of Pecola's parents and the negative impact that their fights have on Pecola and her brother Sammy. As the reader will soon come to expect, the third person narrator is as interested in the *why* as is the first person, Claudia narrator. Without excusing, the narrator explains: without condoning, the narrator understands.

The source of the unhappiness and violence in the family is not the fact that the Breedloves "were poor and black" – that is common in the black community. Rather it lies in the conviction of each member that he/she is ugly, a conviction that *makes* them ugly – it is a vicious circle of self-loathing. To the Breedloves, it seems "as though some mysterious all-knowing master … had said, 'You are ugly people,'" and they see confirmation of this "leaning at them from every billboard, every movie, every glance." In other words, the source of their inferiority complex is the same as that which Claudia has described with reference to Shirley Temple and her white dolls, and just as this led Claudia to feel violent hatred of white girls, so it prompts violence in Mr. and Mrs. Breedlove and Sammy, who project their self-hatred onto others of their color and family rather than against the oppressors as Claudia does.

The narrator tells us that "they took the ugliness in their hands, threw it as a mantle over them, and went about the world with it" because it gives their lives some appearance of meaning and structure (39). Cholly, a violent and cruel man, gets drunk and fights with his wife, which allows him to avoid confronting his own failings; Mrs. Breedlove plays the martyr bearing her husband's wildness and irresponsibility with Christian patience, rather than looking to her own failings. Sammy alternates between joining in the fights on his mother's side and running away. Only the passive Pecola does not react violently, "restricted by youth and sex, [she] experimented with methods of endurance" (43). She hides from the arguments and, engaging in magical thinking, tries to disappear.

Pecola is convinced that, "[a]s long as she looked the way she did, as long as she was ugly, she would have to stay with these people" (45). Having learned from the media that the key to looking beautiful is eye color, she wishes she had blue eyes because then she would be beautiful, and "[i]f she looked different, beautiful, maybe Cholly would be different and Mrs. Breedlove too" (46). Pecola believes that how people *see her* determines how *she sees* the world, and that, if she has blue eyes, people will perceive her as beautiful and she, in turn, will see the world as beautiful. With bitter irony, the narrator comments that, as a result of her conviction, Pecola "would never know her beauty" (46-47). In this, she is typical of most black women in the novel, though for them the consequences are not so disastrous.

There immediately follows an account of an incident which seems to confirm Pecola's view of how the world sees her. As she goes to the grocery store with three pennies to buy candy, she wonders why people consider dandelions ugly because to her their yellow heads are "pretty" (47). Indeed, she feels at home in the world cherishing the mild irritation of the pennies in her sock, the dandelions, the crack in the sidewalk; she feels that she owns these inanimate objects, "And owning them made her part of the world, and the world part of her." She decides to buy Mary Janes (recall that "Jane" is the name of the daughter in the idyllic children's story), but in Mr. Yacobowski, the white store owner, she sees "[t]he total absence of human recognition – the glazed separateness." The narrator explains that this white immigrant has also internalized the white image of female beauty (as epitomized by the images of the Virgin Mary and of Mary Jane on the candy) so that he literally does not "see a little black girl" (48). Worse is to follow because he does not want to take the pennies from Pecola's black hand – another confirmation of the ugliness that comes from being black. Pecola's first reaction is "inexplicable shame" (50), but it is quickly replaced by an anger that she takes out on the dandelions concluding that, "'They are ugly! They are weeds!'" (50). In doing this, she is looking to deflect her own self-loathing; unable any more to trust her own perception of what is beautiful, she succumbs to group-think. Fick explains, "The world is changed because Mr. Yacobowski denies her perspective" (Bloom Ed. *Interpretations Updated* 27). However, in the passive

Pecola anger is succeeded by self-destructive shame. She contrasts the yellow dandelion heads with the yellow wrappers of her nine Mary Janes: now the dandelions look ugly in contrast to the beautiful blue-eyed girl pictured on the candy wrapper, "Smiling white face. Blond hair in gentle disarray, blue eyes looking at her out of a world of clean comfort" (50). Once again the reader notices that whiteness is associated with cleanliness. Pecola partakes of Mary Jane (as she had earlier of Shirley Temple by drinking milk from her cup) in a magical attempt to become the acceptable white ideal of what a girl should be.

The scene with the three whores (Miss Marie [generally called the Maginot Line], China and Poland) provides some comic relief since Pecola evidently has no idea what they actually do. She is amazed that Miss Marie has so many boyfriends and wonders where she gets her money since she "'don't do no work'" (53). On a more serious level, these black women are among the few characters who have no illusions about themselves and who are comfortable with who and what they are. They stir in Pecola a question she has asked before, "What do love feel like? … How do grown-ups act when they love each other? Eat fish together?" Pecola finds it hard to associate the sound of her parents having sex (recall that she and Sammy share their parents' bedroom) with love: Cholly "making sounds as though he were in pain," and her mother making "no noise at all … as though she was not even there." She concludes, "Maybe that was love. Choking sounds and silence" (57).

The names of the whores (the Maginot Line, China and Poland) recall three regions of the world which, in 1941, were falling to either German fascism or Chinese communism, ideologies in which the individual is seen as subservient to the group. This reinforces the point that it is in the proud sense of self (in this case of black self) that the importance of the three whores lies.

Winter

"My daddy's face is a study…"

Questions

15. What impression of Claudia's father is conveyed by the opening paragraph?

16. Exactly why does Claudia dislike Maureen Peal so much?

17. Maureen appears to make friends with Pecola. How does she do this and what is her real motivation for doing so?

18. Explain the humor of the incident in which Mr. Henry treats the two sisters to ice cream.

Commentary

The chapter opens with Claudia's description of her father. He is a commanding and protective figure, a force of nature, a Roman god. He works "night and day" to keep the wolf from the door and makes sure that the house stays warm. Nothing could be a greater contrast with Cholly Breedlove.

Maureen Peal is described as a "high-yellow dream child with long brown hair braided into two lynch ropes that hung down her back" (62). Put simply, she is a mixed-race girl who can pass for white. She is also comparatively rich and very popular at school with both the white and black kids. Claudia and Frieda take an instant dislike her and search for flaws. Seeing the superiority of Maureen's clothes and the ease with which she mixes at school, Claudia tells us, "I wanted to kick her … I plotted accidental slammings of locker doors on her hand," though none of these plans is carried through (63).

As Gillan explains, when the respectable black people of Lorain see Maureen "they focus on her presence and forget the history she represents. They see her ahistorically (i.e., lacking historical perspective or context) as a dream child instead of willing themselves to acknowledge that she is born out of the nightmare of the sexual exploitation of black women justified by a slave-owning culture's hierarchy of racialized personhood" (Bloom. Ed. *Interpretations Updated* 162-163). Through no fault of her own, Maureen is to the reader a living symbol of generations of slave women being raped by their slave masters. Significantly, Claudia as narrator prompts the reader to see Maureen as her contemporaries failed to see her by describing Maureen's "long brown hair [as] braided into two lynch ropes that hung down her back" (62). The reference to lynching reminds us of the brutal subjugation that produced light-skinned, high-yellow dream children like Maureen.

The hostility between the sisters and Maureen seems to evaporate when Maureen offers to walk home with them. Claudia tells the reader, "It was a false spring day," meaning that the day was unseasonably warm, but this detail foreshadows the argument to come (64). By chance, the three girls come upon a gang of boys harassing Pecola by taunting her about two things over which she has "no control": her own black skin and her father sleeping naked (if, indeed, Cholly does sleep naked). With bitter irony, the mature narrator comments, "That they themselves were black, or that their own father had similarly relaxed habits were irrelevant" (65). The boys are projecting their own self-loathing onto the vulnerable Pecola who is an easy victim. Frieda, Claudia and finally Maureen intervene to save Pecola by standing up to the boys. Frieda threatens to reveal that one of the boys still wets his bed.

At first, Maureen's sympathy and friendship for Pecola seem genuine, "Maureen, suddenly animated, put her velvet-sleeved arm through Pecola's and began to behave as though they were the closest of friends" (67). She even treats Pecola (though not Claudia and Frieda) to ice cream. Reluctantly, Claudia concludes, "Maybe she wasn't so bad, after all" (68). Claudia, however, soon reveals Maureen's motivation.

The four girls, each of whom is coming to the end of her childhood, talk about menstruation and its connection to having babies. It is Maureen who initiates the discussion, and it is soon evident why she has befriended Pecola when she asks if Pecola has ever seen a naked man. Pecola replies that she has never seen her father naked. Since Pecola's answer does not answer her question, Maureen presses the issue, and Claudia and Frieda spring to Pecola's defense. Claudia explains their reaction, "we had seen our own father naked and didn't care to be reminded of it and feel the shame brought on by the absence of shame" (71). The reader suspects, however, that in Pecola's case her repeated insistence that she has never seen her father naked will turn out to have a less innocent explanation.

In the resulting argument, Pecola tries to hide, tries magically to disappear, "Pecola tucked her head in … as though she wanted to cover her ears … She seemed to fold into herself, like a pleated wing" (72-73). Maureen retreats back into the superiority of her light complexion. She shouts, "'I *am* cute! And you ugly! Black and ugly e mos. I *am* cute!'" (73). The narrator explains that she and her sister were still young enough to feel "comfortable" in their skins. Nevertheless, what Maureen has said eats away at their self-confidence because, "[i]f she was cute – and if anything could be believed, she *was* – then we were not." This adds to the growth of envy, though the narrator claims, "All the time we knew that Maureen Peel was not the enemy … The *Thing* to fear was the *Thing* that made *her* beautiful, and not us" (74). This judgment has been criticized as hindsight, but surely what Claudia means is that she and her sister sensed this truth at the time, not that they were able to articulate it.

The pervasiveness of the mass media's preference for whiteness is again stressed. When Maureen is trying to ingratiate herself with Pecola, she says that Pecola's name reminds her of the name of the heroine in the movie *Imitation of*

Life (1934), in which the light-skinned daughter of a white man rejects her mother "'because she is black and ugly but then cries at the funeral'" (67). It is important, however, that the Peola (note the spelling) of the movie can easily pass for white whereas the real Pecola cannot: the ideal of white beauty still rules, and it is a standard against which Pecola (and Frieda and Claudia) must always be judged inferior. Maureen's favorite movie star is Betty Grable, but Claudia insists that "'Hedy Lamarr is better'" (69). Maureen tells a story about the absurdly futile attempt of a girl called Audrey to have her hair fixed like Hedy Lamarr's. Having delivered the hairdresser's punch line, ""'Yeah, when you grow some hair like Hedy Lamarr's,'"" Maureen "laughed long and sweet" (70). Each of these three references shows Maureen's preference for white skin and her willingness to direct her own resentment that she is not white against those who are darker than she is. They also show the futility of black women aspiring to look like white women.

As we have seen, Pecola is hurt by Maureen's behavior, but though they are angered by it, Claudia and Frieda are not emotionally damaged. Claudia explains that the reason was that she and her sister have no self-loathing. On the contrary, they feel comfortable in their black skin, "Guileless and without vanity, we were still in love with ourselves then. We … enjoyed the news that our senses released to us, admired our dirt, cultivated our scars…" (74). They feel no envy of whites because they feel no unworthiness at being black. Notice, however, that Claudia's use of verb tenses implies that, as they grew up, they learned to feel shame and envy – just as she learned to love Shirley Temple.

In another comic interlude, the girls' naivety on matters relating to sex is exposed. Mr. Henry gives them money for ice cream, but it is only because he is entertaining the prostitutes China and the Maginot Line (Miss Marie) in the living room. When she and her sister return, Claudia sees Henry with the women, though she is too young to understand what is going on, she finds herself reacting sexually. However, the sisters accept his lies that the women are members of his Bible-study group. They decide to keep his secret because telling their mother would only make her "'fuss all day'" – something they will do anything to avoid (79).

SEETHECATITGOES…

Questions

19. Explain your understanding of the term "funkiness." Why must women like Geraldine repress the funkiness that is a part of their nature?

20. In what way has Junior been bullied by his mother? Why does he become a bully?

21. Why does Geraldine immediately believe her son's accusation against Pecola?

Commentary

This chapter describes young black women who have moved north from towns in the South. These women regard themselves as 'colored' not 'niggers,' the difference, in their eyes being that "[c]olored people were neat and quiet; niggers were dirty and loud." They insist that the two are "easily distinguishable," yet are constantly aware that, "[t]he line between colored and nigger was not always clear; subtle and tell-tale signs threatened to erode it, and the watch had to be constant" (87).

These Southern young black women are clean and smell nice:

> They wash themselves with orange-colored
> Lifebuoy soap, dust themselves with Cashmere
> Bouquet talc, clean their teeth with salt on a
> piece of rag, soften their skin with Jergens
> Lotion ... straighten their hair with Dixie
> Peach... (82)

These are the educated black women, but they have only been taught, the narrator tells us, "to do the white man's work with refinement." They have learned white manners and grace and, above all, they have successfully suppressed the "dreadful funkiness of passion the funkiness of nature, the funkiness of the wide range of human emotions" – in a word their blackness (83). They marry and rule over their husbands, but they have no passion for them: during sex, "she will give him her body sparingly and partially" and experience no orgasm, though she will "pretend" to do so (84). They feel more physical pleasure in caressing their cat than in touching their husbands and they bring up their single child strictly and lovelessly catering only to his/her physical needs. (Since these women are attempting to recreate the idyllic white family, it is important to remember the description of Jane's family in the children's book for there too it was empathy and emotion that were lacking between Jane and her parents.)

Geraldine is such a young woman, married to Louis, with a son named Junior who is starved of any real affection such as that which is reserved for the family cat. Geraldine's middle-class pride in having a clean and orderly house and her antipathy to dirt and disorder is linked to her hatred of "niggers" – she hates her own funky blackness. (In contrast, we have seen that Claudia and Frieda take great pleasure in getting dirty and rather resent having to get a bath.) Junior wears white shirts and his hair is cut close "to avoid any suggestion of wool, the part etched into his hair." He has had all of his "funkiness" suppressed. When he was younger he "used to long to play with the black boys ... and have them push him down the mound of dirt and roll him over. He wanted ... to smell their wild blackness..." (87), but his mother has taught him to despise such desires. As a result, Junior hates himself, but he projects that hatred onto others and becomes a bully. That is why Junior tricks

Pecola into coming into his house, throws the cat in her face, and finally hurls it against the window killing it. Discovered by his mother, Geraldine, Junior accuses Pecola of killing the cat. Geraldine immediately believes him for Pecola represents everything about her own blackness that she has sought to escape, "dirty torn dress ... hair matted ... muddy shoes ... soiled socks" (91). To Geraldine, Pecola symbolizes the poor, uneducated blacks with whom she was familiar at home; she represents every African-American characteristic that stands for the vileness of being black. Geraldine calls Pecola a "'nasty little black bitch'" and orders her out of the house (92). The snowflakes that Pecola sees "falling and dying on the pavement" symbolize how devastated she is by what has happened.

One thing that Pecola will remember, however, is that the black cat had blue eyes, "The blue eyes in the black face held her" (90).

Spring

"The first twigs are thin…"

Questions

22. Describe the tone of the section dealing with Mr. Henry's assault on Frieda and its immediate aftermath.

23. What do Claudia and Frieda think that being "ruined" means? Why do they think that (i.e., what is their reasoning)?

24. Can you explain the way in which Mrs. Breedlove treats her own daughter after Pecola drops the blueberry cobbler? Contrast it with the way that she treats the daughter of her employer.

Commentary

Spring arrives, but for Claudia the season is "shot through with the remembered ache of switchings" because in spring the new shoots on the bushes are "thin, green and supple" (98). This opening foreshadows something ominous.

The theme of sex reappears when Claudia finds Frieda upstairs crying and her sister reluctantly tells her that Mr. Henry touched her breasts and that her father "'beat him up.'" Since Frieda was not actually hurt, Claudia extracts comedy from the behavior of her younger self. She asks Frieda if she felt anything when Mr. Henry touched her and is disappointed when her sister tells her, "'It didn't feel like anything'" because Claudia knows it is "'supposed to'" feel good. Next she wants all of the details, after which she complains that she, who is "'tired of having everything last,'" will never have breasts worth a man pinching. Claudia's jealousy that her sister has had a sexual experience before her is comic. When she hears about the Mr. Henry's beating, she is again disappointed saying, "'Oh, shoot, I always miss stuff'" (100). The description of Mr. and Mrs. MacTeer's attack on Mr. Henry is pure slapstick which, of course, is only possible because no one really gets hurt.

The discussion becomes even more comic when Frieda reports the remark of a neighbor, Miss Dunion, that Frieda's parents should take her to the doctor because she might be "ruined" (by which the neighbor means no longer a virgin or even pregnant). Frieda has been crying because, although she has no idea what being "ruined" really means, she does know that it is a bad thing. As far as Frieda and Claudia can work it out, being "ruined" means that Frieda will become fat like the Miss Marie (the Maginot Line). As the Sparknotes editors explain, "not understanding what makes the prostitute distasteful to their mother, they focus on what makes the prostitute distasteful to them – her fatness." Claudia suggests that her sister can "'exercise and not eat'" to prevent herself from getting fat. It then strikes her that China and Poland are "ruined" but not fat because "'Mama said whiskey ate them up'" (101). Clearly Frieda needs to drink whiskey to avoid the physical signs of being "ruined" which they decide they can get from Pecola because her father is always drunk. The comic irony of the perfect logic of the sisters leading to an absurd conclusion provides light relief.

At Pecola's house, Claudia and Frieda encounter Miss Marie who invites them inside. Claudia notes that "her smile was full, not like the pinched and holding-back smile of other grown-ups" (103), another indication of the price in human spontaneity that the respectable blacks pay for their respectability. When Frieda tells her that they are not allowed to visit her because their mother says she is "ruined," Miss Marie throws a bottle at them and laughs. Such spontaneous behavior is unnerving to the sisters. They still have not the faintest idea what the word means because they have not the faintest idea what a prostitute is. When they finally find Pecola she stoutly defends Miss Marie and China and Poland who are all very kind and generous to her. It is possible for Claudia to present the events of this chapter as comedy because Frieda was not seriously assaulted, her parents acted quickly to protect her, and the incident did no long-term damage. In fact, Claudia has already told the reader that the two girls have fond memories of Henry despite what he did.

The comedy is, however, prelude to a scene with much more serious implications. Mrs. Breedlove is working at one of the big houses near Lake Shore Park on Lake Erie where black people are not allowed to go despite the fact that it is a "public park." The park epitomizes the association of being white with cleanliness and good order, "It was empty now, but sweetly expectant of clean, white, well-behaved children and parents who play there..." (105). The house itself is also well ordered, "The walkway was flagged in calculated disorder, hiding the cunning symmetry" (106). This is the kind of house and the kind of life to which blacks like Geraldine aspire and attempt to emulate. Claudia notices the "white porcelain, white woodwork ... white swinging door" (107-108).

Claudia is shocked and angry when one of the white children calls Pecola's mother "Polly." Claudia recalls, "The familiar violence rose in me. Her calling Mrs. Breedlove Polly, when even Pecola called her mother Mrs. Breedlove, seemed reason enough to scratch her" (108). This seems to her to be another example of a white person disrespecting a black person. Worse is to follow, for when Pecola accidentally pulls a freshly baked berry cobbler off the counter, in the process burning her legs so badly that she cries with pain, her mother's only concern seems to be for the mess her daughter has made on her clean floor. She hits Pecola "with the back of her hand [and] knocked her to the floor," then continues slapping her and telling her off "in a voice thin with anger." In contrast, when the "little girl in pink" starts to cry, Mrs. Breedlove offers her the tender reassurance that she ought to have shown her daughter (109). If

Pecola's father rapes her, here her own mother fails to acknowledge her relationship with her and fails in her duty of care. (Compare, "See Mother. Mother is very nice. Mother, will you play with Jane? Mother laughs. Laugh, Mother, laugh" [3].)

The one lasting impression that the sisters take from this day is the superiority of whites. Lake Shore Park is an up-scale white neighborhood where everything is well kept. The house they enter is magnificent, unlike anything they have ever seen. (Pecola had a similar reaction to Geraldine's house when she entered it.) It is a completely different world. The little white girl (almost a carbon copy of Shirley Temple) is dressed in delicate pink and has yellow hair. Pecola spills "blackish blueberries" all over the floor, underlining the connection between blackness and mess. Ironically, her mother is more concerned about her dirty floor (the floor is, of course, only *hers* in the sense that she has cleaned it for a white family) than she is about the fact that her daughter has been burned by the hot berries. When she speaks to Pecola and the sisters, her voice is like "rotten pieces of apple," but when she speaks to the white girl, "the honey in her words complemented the sundown spilling on the lake" (109). When the white girl asks who the black children were Mrs. Breedlove avoids identifying her own daughter. As Awkward explains, her "refusal to share with the white girl Pecola's identity [is] because of her shame at being identified with the clumsy, pathetic girl who knocks the blueberry pie onto the floor" (Bloom Ed. *Interpretations* 86). Pauline's allegiance to her own black family is placed second to her allegiance to the family of her white employer.

SEEMOTHERMOTHERISVERYNICE...

Questions

25. Pauline blames the death of her dreams on the accident to her foot, but the narrator thinks that the real cause was "the cavity in one of her front teeth" (110). Evaluate these two possibilities.

26. Why was Pauline never as happy in Lorain, Ohio, as she had been in Alabama or even Kentucky?

27. What lessons does Pauline learn from the movies? How does her view of her life and her *self* change as a result?

28. Compare and/or contrast Pauline's experience of sex with Cholly with Geraldine's experience of sex with her husband.

Commentary

This chapter tells the story of Pecola's mother, Pauline Williams. It explains how she came to be the woman that the reader has just seen treat her own daughter so unfairly. For the first time in the novel, the author employs a double perspective alternating a third person omniscient narrator with Pauline's own stream of consciousness account of her life. The result is that the reader begins to understand the forces that molded Mrs. Breedlove's character. Her story traces her movement away from the organic black community into which she was born toward white middle-class values which require her to destroy her *self* and remake herself in the image of the dominant culture – an enterprise in which she is doomed to fail from the start. Her life and character are partly the result of events beyond her control, like getting a nail through her foot when she was two, and partly the result of choices she has freely made, like going to the movies.

Pauline was born in Alabama and later moved with her family to Kentucky. She grew up as an isolated child because of a slight foot deformity but had a natural talent for housekeeping and took great joy in putting things in order. The most poignant statement is the narrator's assertion that, as a child, Pauline "missed, without knowing that she missed – paints and crayons" which suggests that her potentially artistic temperament was never nurtured (111). The joys of her life she remembers in terms of colors: the streak of green made by the June bugs on the night her family left Alabama; the yellow of her mother's lemonade; and the purple of the berries that stained her dress one Sunday. Pauline fell in love with Cholly Breedlove and she describes the feeling as "*like them berries, that lemonade, them streaks of green the june bugs made, all come together*" (115). She describes their lovemaking in terms of the same colors. As she orgasms, she writes that "*I begin to feel those little bits of color floating up into me – deep in me ... it be rainbow all inside.*" The reader can have no doubt why Pauline loved Cholly, nor why she stayed with him even after he began drinking. Now that there is no love left in the marriage she writes, "*Only think I miss sometimes is that rainbow. But, like I say, I don't recollect it much anymore*" (131). The truthfulness of that last statement is undermined by the sexual detail of the previous few pages. Unlike Geraldine, who never attains an orgasm because she will not give herself to her husband sufficiently, the orgasms that Pauline attained with Cholly were some of the most beautiful and meaningful experiences of her life.

Pauline and Cholly married and moved north to Lorain, Ohio, where Cholly got a job and the two were happy for some years, but by the time Pauline became pregnant the marriage was on the slide, though there were still times when their lovemaking brought them together. Feeling isolated because "*It was hard to get to know folks up here, and I missed my people*" (117), Pauline found refuge in the movie theaters where she saw:

> White men taking such good care of they
> women, and they all dressed up in big clean
> houses with the bathtubs right in the same
> room with the toilet. (123)

Clearly nothing that she could do would make her own life like that, and so she began to give up on managing her own household. The movies also introduced her to romantic love and to a white ideal of physical beauty which the narrator calls, "Probably the most destructive ideas in the history of human thought. Both originated in envy, thrived in insecurity, and ended in disillusion." She "absorbed in full" the "scale of absolute beauty" that the movies presented and applied it to every face she saw, including her own (122). Ironically, it was at the movies, with her hair set to look like Jean Harlow's, that Pauline lost a front tooth, an accident which convinced her that she could never aspire to the white ideal of "absolute beauty" (122). She admits, "*Everything went then*" (123). Without being aware of it, she comes to think of herself (and later of her daughter) as ugly. Of the decay of the tooth, the narrator comments that "even before the little brown speck [of tooth decay], there must have been the conditions, the setting that would allow it to exist in the first place" (116). By this she means that the loss of the tooth was just the culmination of everything in Pauline's life that had made her hate her own blackness. Gillan explains, "Pauline imagines that her inability to be beautiful or stylish stems from some inherent fault; in so doing, she fails to account for the economic barriers to her attainment of the privileged homemaker position in one of those white houses" (Bloom Ed. *Interpretations Update* 169). Of course, even if she had had this perspective, she would have been helpless to do anything about it.

A second baby, Pecola, failed to improve matters. In the hospital, when she was about to give birth to Pecola, Pauline encountered pervasive white racism. The doctor in charge announced to the doctors in training that she was "one of these here women you don't have any trouble with. They deliver right away with no pain. Just like horses" (124-125). Pauline was outraged by this racist stereotyping (and, as a country girl, by his lack of knowledge about horses), but it all formed her into a mother who described her daughter oxymoronically, "She looked like a black ball of hair ... But I knowed she was ugly. Head full of pretty hair, but Lord she was ugly" (124, 126). Here the reader can literally see the two influences driving Pauline's judgment: the natural love of a mother, which is emotion, and the "absolute scale of beauty," which is rational.

Cholly was by now a hopeless drunk. Pauline joined the church which allowed her access to the company of the respectable ladies of the black community. Significantly, we are told that she "joined a church where shouting was frowned upon," that is, a church which looks down on black passion and mimics white restraint. Here she consciously eradicated her southern accent, "She stopped saying chil'ren' and said 'childring' instead" (126), so that the black women who had disdained her when she first came to Lorain now accepted her. The church also encouraged her to project her own self-loathing onto her sinful husband. Finding her own household irredeemably ugly and quite beyond her power to beautify, she transferred all of her attention to the

Fisher household, "Soon she stopped trying to keep her own house. The things she could afford to buy did not last, had no beauty or style, and were absorbed into the dingy storefront." The Fishers are a wealthy white family and in their fine house Pauline, now Polly, can take pride in her work, "Here she found beauty, order, cleanliness, and praise" (127). Here she finds her life to be meaningful. Pauline likes the nickname she is given, but the reader understands that it suggests that she parrots (i.e., repeats) what she has been taught about the superiority of everything white.

The pseudo-white world that Geraldine creates in her middle-class home, Pauline experiences vicariously in the Fishers' home. Each woman brings up her children to "respectability" as it is defined by middle-class whites. The effect on Sammy is similar to the effect on Junior: he hates everything about his life and just wants to run away (just as Cholly did). However in Pecola the effect is to produce "a fear of growing up, fear of other people, fear of life" (128).

"SEEFATHERHEISBIGANDSTRONG..."

Questions

29. Cholly Breedlove's life is a succession of humiliations. As you read the chapter, make a list of these and comment on their effects on him.

30. Explain why Cholly hates Darlene so much for what happens when they have sex in the field.

31. How does Cholly change after having been rejected by his father?

32. Why does Cholly have sex with his own daughter?

Commentary

Frieda's experience of Mr. Henry's unwanted sexual attentions contrasts sharply with the experience of Pecola. Whereas Frieda is not physically harmed (and appears not to have been emotionally harmed since Claudia has informed the reader that "Even after what came later, there was no bitterness in our memory of him" [16]) by Mr. Henry's groping, Pecola is raped; whereas Frieda's father takes effective action to protect her, Pecola's father is himself the perpetrator. In the prologue, Claudia tells us that "in the fall of 1941 ... Pecola was having her father's baby" (5). In this chapter the third person omniscient narrator (interestingly Cholly is given no voice) describes how Cholly came to the point at which he raped his daughter: it does not excuse or even mitigate the crime, but it does explain it. The Sparknotes Editors put it much better than I can, "Cholly's violence is not frightening because it is senseless; it is frightening because it makes all too much sense, given the kind of life he has lived." It is not possible for the reader to judge what Cholly did other than in the context of a lifetime of being poor and victimized by both blacks and whites.

Cholly Breedlove suffered a succession of humiliations. He was illegitimate; his mother, who "wasn't right in the head," abandoned him on a junk heap and ran off soon afterward (132); and his father disappeared before he was born. Indeed, it is not even possible to identify his father with certainty because, as Great Aunt Jimmy told him, it could have been the "'Fuller boy [Samson] ... Him or his brother. Maybe both'" (133). Aunt Jimmy raised him, but "took great delight sometimes in telling him how she had saved him" so that sometimes he wished he had been left to die on the junk heap (132). As a young man, his conception of God was of:

> a nice old white man, with long white hair,
> flowing white beard and little blue eyes that
> looked sad when people died and mean when
> they were bad.

Finding nothing in this image with which to identify, Cholly preferred "the strong, black devil" (134).

The gathering of old women at the death of Aunt Jimmy provides the narrator with the opportunity to explain the double powerlessness of black women:

> Everyone in the world was in a position to give
> them orders. White women said, "Do this."
> White children said, "Give me that." White
> men said, "Come here." Black men said, "Lay
> down." (138)

Nevertheless, these women achieved great things, and the narrator celebrates them. The gathering of such women and the ceremonies that they perform related to Aunt Jimmy's laying out and funeral give the reader a glimpse into the organic black culture which still exists in the South, but which will be shown to be entirely absent in northern towns like Lorain. Aunt Jimmy, however, dies without leaving "'even a pocket handkerchief.'" Her house, which she might at some time have owned "'belongs to some white folks in Clarksville'" (142).

Cholly had his first hostile encounter with whites when two armed hunters discovered him having sex for the first time in the fields. Initially, Cholly was gentle with Darlene, assuring her. "'You ain't dirty'" and carefully trying to retie her hair ribbon. However, when the hunters made him continue having sex with Darleen while they watched and laughed, the narrator says, "With a violence born of total helplessness, he pulled her dress up, lowered his trousers and underwear... He hated her. He almost wished he could do it – hard, long, and painfully, he hated her so much" (148). Cholly projected all of his anger against the white men onto the girl because she was "the one who had created the situation, the one who bore witness to his failure, his impotence. The one he had not been able to protect" (151). This is how the projection of self-hatred works, "Never once did he consider directing his hatred toward the hunters. Such an emotion would destroy him. They were big, white, armed men. He was small, black, helpless" (150). His feelings are different only in intensity from those of Junior and Maureen, both bullies who hurt others for inadequacies that they perceive, but cannot acknowledge, in themselves.

Perhaps Cholly's greatest humiliation was his failed attempt to reconnect with the man he believed to be his father, Samson Fuller. He traveled to Macon and located the man but was rejected by him. Carmean explains the defining impact of this rejection on Cholly:

> Morrison indicates the profound injury his father's lack of interest inflicts on Cholly through Cholly's immediate withdrawal to infantilism, first he soils himself and soon after when he draws himself into the fetal position under a river pier. A reborn Cholly emerges from the water... (23)

From this point on, the narrator tells us, "Cholly was free. Dangerously free. Free to feel whatever he felt – fear, guilt, shame, love grief, pity" (159). He no longer had a family or a community to which he belonged (both of which would have moderated his behavior) and alternated between violence (killing three white men) and tenderness (as when he first met Pauline).

Though he loved Pauline, marriage to one woman made him feel trapped, "The constantness, varietylessness, the sheer weight of sameness drove him to despair and froze his imagination." He lost interest in life and began to drink. When children came, never having had a father himself, he had no idea how to relate to them. Being a father "dumbfounded him and rendered him totally dysfunctional" (160). Unable to form a "stable connection" between himself and his children, "his reactions were based on what he felt at the moment." One day, he comes home drunk to find Pecola doing the dishes and the sight generates a sequence of emotions "revulsion, guilt, pity, then love" (161). That is when he rapes her – she is eleven. Awkward argues that it is possible to see Cholly's action "as his attempt to relieve the persistent pain of the ignominy of his own sexual initiation by involving his daughter in an even more ignominious sexual act" (Bloom. Ed. *Interpretations* 88).

"SEETHEDOGBOWWOW..."

Questions

33. Explain how Soaphead's ancestors systematically sought to eliminate traces of their black heritage.

34. Explain why Soaphead chooses to satisfy his sexual urges with young girls.

35. What is Soaphead's view of God and His creation?

36. Does Soaphead simply manipulate Pecola (using her to kill a dog he hates) or is there more to what he does?

Commentary

This chapter tells the history of the strangely named Soaphead Church (aka Elihue Micah Whitcomb), a self-declared "Reader, Adviser, and Interpreter of Dreams" in Lorain's black community. Pecola comes to ask him to give her blue eyes, and he tricks her into poisoning his landlady's old dog which he has long hated.

Soaphead is a "cinnamon-eyed West Indian with lightly browned skin" who is descended from an English gentleman who, in the early 1880's, "introduced the white strain into the family." This gentleman's bastard child married a similarly mixed-race girl who "like a Victorian parody, learned from her husband all that was worth learning – to separate herself in mind, body, and spirit from all that suggested Africa." Down the generations, the family was "proud of its academic accomplishments and its mixed blood – in fact they believed the former to be based on the latter" (167). With a very few exceptions, family members "married 'up,' lightening the family complexion and thinning out the family features" (198).

Early in his life, Soaphead developed a revulsion against dirt and a disgust of human physicality, "He abhorred flesh on flesh. Body odor, breathe odor, overwhelmed him" (166). He had, "A hatred of, and fascination with, any hint of disorder and decay" (169). That left him isolated and lonely. When he met and married Velma, he was convinced that he had found "the answer to his unstated, unacknowledged question – where was the life to counter the encroaching non-life?" but the marriage ended after two months when Velma simply walked away. We are told, "He never got over her desertion" (170). Since he was, despite his distaste for physical contact, subject to sexual urges, Soaphead directed his attentions toward young girls "humans whose bodies were least offensive" (166). The Sparknote Editors write that "his obsession with bodily purity has made him more perverted than simple lust would have." That perversion is clearly related to the white obsession with order and cleanliness. With bitter irony, the third person narrator comments, "his patronage of little girls smacked of innocence, and was associated in his mind with cleanliness. He was what one might call a very clean old man" (166-167). All of this explains why, when Pecola comes to him with her request for blue eyes, Soaphead's own attraction to whiteness makes her wish easily comprehensible to him. He immediately considers it both "the most fantastic and the most logical petition he had ever received. Here was an ugly little girl asking for beauty" (174).

After Pecola has run away from the dying dog, Soaphead writes a letter to

44

God which is full of self-justification. Aware that "decay, vice, filth, and disorder were pervasive" in the world, he has long ago come to the conclusion that "Evil existed because God had created it. He, God, had made a sloven and unforgivable error in judgment: designing an imperfect universe" (172). Pecola's brown eyes seem to him just the latest of a series of errors made by God. He blames God for everything, beginning with the fact that his Caribbean ancestors "took as [their] own the most dramatic, and the most obvious of our white masters' characteristics, which were, of course, their worst" (177). Here Soaphead shows tremendous perception about the degrading influence of the desire to reject blackness and imitate whiteness which has been a constant theme of the novel. He excuses his abuse of young girls, blaming God for allowing it to happen and for making their little breasts so lovely that "I couldn't … keep my hands my mouth, off them" (179). He accuses God of ignoring Pecola's wish for blue eyes so that she had to come to a man like him. He asserts, "I did what you did not, would not, could not do: I looked at that ugly little black girl, and I loved her. I played You. And it was a very good show!" (182). He believes that he has performed a miracle: Pecola will have blue eyes, though only she will be able to see them.

Summer

"I have only to break..."

Questions

37. What motivates Claudia and Frieda to want to save Pecola's baby?

38. Explain what Claudia means when she writes, "Our limitations were not known to us – not then" (189).

Commentary

Through piecing together overheard conversations, Claudia and Frieda learn that Pecola is pregnant by her father who has run away. They also learn that when Mrs. Breedlove found out what had happened she beat Pecola severely. The sisters know that having a baby when you are unmarried is wrong, but they also know that it is quite common. They have no conception of incest because "the process of having a baby by any male was incomprehensible to us" (190-191). The neighborhood gossips blame Pecola, "'She carry some blame ... How come she didn't fight him?'" (189). Everyone seems to want the baby to die because (although they are not conscious of this) to them it represents the worst aspects of blackness, "'Ought to be a law; two ugly people doubling up like that to make more ugly. Be better off in the ground'" (190). Claudia is horrified by "this overwhelming hatred for the unborn baby" (191). Instinctively, she sees that the opinions of the respectable black women are informed by their acceptance of the absolute standards of white beauty:

> More strongly than my fondness for Pecola, I
> felt a need for someone to want the black baby
> to live – just to counteract the universal love of
> white baby dolls, Shirley Temples, and
> Maureen Peels.

Claudia envisages the baby in Pecola's womb, and her description stresses the baby's blackness:

> It was in a dark, wet place, its head covered
> with great O's of wool, the black face holding,
> like nickels, two clean black eyes, the flared
> nose, kissing-thick lips, and the living
> breathing silk of black skin. (190)

Claudia and Frieda, engaging in magical thinking, decide to help Pecola and the baby by praying, sacrificing their seed money and the bicycle it would buy, and planting the remaining marigold seeds. However, as Awkward explains, "The planting of seeds in *The Bluest Eye* serves to demonstrate not nature's harmony with humanity and the possibility of preserving (at least the memory of) life, but, rather, a barren earth's indifference to humanity's needs" (Bloom Ed. *Interpretations* 99).

"LOOKLOOKHERECOMES…"

Questions

39. Who is Pecola's friend?

40. Who does Claudia blame for what happened to Pecola? Do you agree?

Commentary

Certain facts emerge: Pecola was raped twice by her father, once in the kitchen and once when she was on the sofa; she no longer goes to school; Cholly and Sammy have left home; Pecola still lives with her mother who has moved to a house on the edge of town; and Mrs. Breedlove still works for the Fishers.

The dialogue is between Pecola and an imaginary friend (the voice in italics). The dialogue seems surreal. The reader observes the way in which Pecola is still trying to make sense of what she has experienced: her consciousness has divided to produce an imaginary friend. The friend says that Mrs. Breedlove had sex with Cholly a lot and concludes, "*she probably loved him anyway,*" but Pecola denies this asserting that "he made her" (198). The friend also wants to know if having sex with her father was "horrible," even the second time, but Pecola simply gets angry. Perhaps the friend is right and Pecola did find something in the physical experience enjoyable about which she is now ashamed.

The main topic of conversations is, however, Pecola's blue eyes. She keeps looking at them in the mirror and admiring them, but she also needs her friend's constant reassurance that they are blue, indeed, that they are the bluest eyes. She worries that, "If there is somebody with bluer eyes than mine, then maybe there is somebody with the bluest eyes. The bluest eyes in the whole world" (203). Pecola desperately wants to be that person.

Claudia resumes the narrative, but it is no longer a narrative that limits itself to a child's understanding. The mature Claudia has knowledge of events (for example, Pecola's dream of having blue eyes) and the ability to evaluate them that were previously limited to the third person omniscient narrator. Sadly, she records Pecola's descent into madness:

> A little black girl yearns for the blue eyes of a
> little white girl, and the horror at the heart of
> her yearning is exceeded only by the evil of
> fulfillment. (204)

The understanding of the significance of the way the community reacted to Pecola's pregnancy that the mature Claudia shows is perhaps the only good thing to come out of Pecola's tragedy. She understands that Pecola has been made into a scapegoat by the community (herself included) which exorcised its own self-loathing by destroying her:

> We were so beautiful when we stood astride
> her ugliness ... We honed our egos on her,
> padded out characters with her frailty, and
> yawned in the fantasy of our strength. (205)

Claudia understands that Pecola is the last and most damaged of many victims of projection in the novel. As Gravett concludes:

> As long as people are able to bear witness to
> the failures of society and are unafraid to speak
> or write the truths they perceive, perhaps hope
> does still exist for the future. Since Claudia has
> survived to tell her story, maybe her seeds have
> not failed after all. (Bloom Ed. *Interpretations
> Updated* 94)

Perspectives

Consider these verdicts on the novel:

This is a desolate novel. There is no mistaking the pitifulness and hopelessness of the story. If as we read we try to find solace in some imagined growth of Frieda and Claudia, then we are mistaken. (Holloway Bloom. Ed. *Interpretations* 35)

The Bluest Eye is an angry book but it is also an orderly one... (Fick, Bloom. Ed. *Interpretations Updated* 20).

As imperfect as Cholly is, he is still more genuine than Pauline. His rape of Pecola is reprehensible, but he does not rape her mind the way Pauline and Soaphead do. (Alexander, Bloom. Ed. *Interpretations Updated* 122).

Annotated Bibliography

Morrison, Toni. *The Bluest Eye*. 1970. New York: First Vintage International Edition, 2007. Print.

Bloom, Harold. Ed. *Modern Critical Interpretations: Toni Morrison's "The Bluest Eye"*. Philadelphia: Chelsea House Publishers, 1999. Print.
(An excellent collection of essays most of which are well written and accessible to the general reader.)

Bloom, Harold. Ed. *Bloom's Modern Critical Interpretations: Toni Morrison's "The Bluest Eye" Updated Edition.* New York: Infobase Publishing, 2007. Print.
(This edition retains three of the original essays but the majority of the essays are more recent. Most are well written and accessible to the general reader.)

Carmean, Karen. *Toni Morrison's World of Fiction*. Troy: The Whitson Publishing Company, 1993. Print.
(I assume that this book has been revised and up-dated. The introduction and the chapter on *The Bluest Eye* are well worth reading.)

SparkNotes Editors. *SparkNote on "The Bluest Eye"*. SparkNotes.com. SparkNotes LLC. 2002. Web. 6 Apr. 2017.
(I found this source incredibly helpful and recommend it.)

Literary terms activity

As you use each term in the study guide, fill in the definition of the term and include an example from the text to show how it is used. The first definition is supplied. Find an example in the text to complete it.

Term	Definition
	Example
Antagonist	*a character or force opposing the protagonist.*
Climax	
Dialogue	
First person	
Foreshadow	

Term	Definition
	Example
Genre	
Image/imagery	
Imply, implication	
Irony. ironic	
Literally	
Motivation/ motivate	

The Bluest Eye by Toni Morrison

Term	Definition
	Example
Narrator	
Narrative	
Oxymoron	
Perspective	
Plot	
Prologue	

A Study Guide

Term	Definition
	Example
Protagonist	
Realism	
Setting	
Symbol/ symbolic/ symbolism/ symbolize	
Theme	
Third person	

The Bluest Eye by Toni Morrison

Term	Definition
	Example
Tone	
Tragic	

Literary terms

NOTE: Not every one of these terms will be relevant to this particular study guide

Allegorical: a story in which the characters, their actions and the settings represent abstract ideas (often moral ideas) or historical/political events.

Ambiguous, ambiguity: when a statement is unclear in meaning – ambiguity may be deliberate or accidental.

Analogy: a comparison which treats two things as identical in one or more specified ways.

Antagonist: a character or force opposing the protagonist.

Antithesis: the complete opposite of something.

Authorial comment: when the writer addresses the reader directly (not to be confused with the narrator doing so).

Climax: the conflict to which the action has been building since the start of the play or story.

Colloquialism: the casual, informal mainly spoken language of ordinary people – often called "slang."

Comic hyperbole: deliberately inflated, extravagant language used for comic effect.

Comic Inversion: reversing the normally accepted order of things for comic effect.

Connotation: the ideas, feelings and associations generated by a word or phrase.

Dark comedy: comedy which has a serious implication – comedy that deals with subjects not usually treated humorously (e.g., death).

Dialogue: a conversation between two or more people in direct speech.

Diction: the writer's choice of words in order to create a particular effect.

Equivocation: saying something which is capable of two interpretations with the intention of misrepresenting the truth.

Euphemism: a polite word for an ugly truth – for example, a person is said to be sleeping when they are actually dead.

Fallacy: a misconception resulting from incorrect reasoning.

First person: first person singular is "I" and plural is "we".

Foreshadow: a statement or action which gives the reader a hint of what is likely to happen later in the narrative.

Form of speech: the register in which speech is written – the diction reflects the character.

Frame narrative: a story within which the main narrative is placed.

Genre: the type of literature into which a particular text falls (e.g. drama, poetry, novel).

Hubris: pride – in Greek tragedy it is the hero's belief that he can challenge the will of the gods.

Hyperbole: exaggeration designed to create a particular effect.

Image, imagery: figurative language such as simile, metaphor, personification etc., or a description which conjures up a particularly vivid picture.

Imply, implication: when the text suggests to the reader a meaning which it does not actually state.

Infer, inference: the reader's act of going beyond what is stated in the text to draw conclusions.

Irony, ironic: a form of humor which undercuts the apparent meaning of a statement:

> *Conscious irony:* irony used deliberately by a writer or character;
>
> *Unconscious irony:* a statement or action which has significance for the reader of which the character is unaware;
>
> *Dramatic irony*: when an action has an important significance that is obvious to the reader but not to one or more of the characters;
>
> *Tragic irony:* when a character says (or does) something which will have a serious, even fatal, consequence for him/ her. The audience is aware of the error, but the character is not;
>
> *Verbal irony*: the conscious use of particular words which are appropriate to what is being said.

Juxtaposition: literally putting two things side by side for purposes of comparison and/ or contrast.

Literal: the surface level of meaning that a statement has.

Melodramatic: action and/or dialogue that is inflated or extravagant – frequently used for comic effect.

Metaphor, metaphorical: the description of one thing by direct comparison with another (e.g. the coal-black night).

> *Extended metaphor:* a comparison which is developed at length.

Microcosm: literally 'the world is little' – a situation which reflects truths about the world in general.

Mood: the feelings and emotions contained in and/ or produced by a work of art (text, painting, music, etc.).

Motif: a frequently repeated idea, image or situation in a text.

Motivation: why a character acts as he/she does – in modern literature motivation is seen as psychological.

Narrator: the voice that the reader hears in the text – not to be confused with the author.

> *Frame narrative /story:* a story within which the main story is told (e.g. *Heart of Darkness* by Conrad begins with five men on a boat in the Thames and then one of them tells the story of his experiences on the river Congo).

Oxymoron: the juxtaposition of two terms normally thought of as opposite (e.g. the silent scream).

Parable: a story with a moral lesson (e.g. the Good Samaritan).

Paradox, paradoxical: a statement or situation which appears self-contradictory and therefore absurd.

Pathos: is pity, or rather the ability of a text to make the audience or reader feel pity.

Perspective: point of view from which a story, or an incident within a story, is told.

Personified, personification: a simile or metaphor in which an inanimate object or abstract idea is described by comparison with a human.

Plot: a chain of events linked by cause and effect.

Prologue: an introduction which gives a lead-in to the main story.

Protagonist: the character who initiates the action and is most likely to have the sympathy of the audience.

Pun: a deliberate play on words where a particular word has two or more meanings both appropriate in some way to what is being said.

Realism: a text that describes the action in a way that appears to reflect life.

Rhetoric: any use of language designed to make the expression of ideas more effective (e.g. repetition, imagery, alliteration, etc.).

Sarcasm: stronger than irony – it involves a deliberate attack on a person or idea with the intention of mocking.

Satire, Satiric: the use of comedy to criticize attack, belittle, or humiliate – more extreme than irony.

Setting: the environment in which the narrative (or part of the narrative) takes place.

Simile: a description of one thing by explicit comparison with another (e.g. my love is like a red, red rose).

> *Extended simile*: a comparison which is developed at length.

Style: the way in which a writer chooses to express him/ herself. Style is a vital aspect of meaning since how something is expressed can crucially affect what is being written or spoken.

Suspense: the building of tension in the reader.

Symbol, symbolic, symbolism, symbolize: a physical object which comes to represent an abstract idea (e.g. the sun may symbolize life).

Themes: important concepts, beliefs and ideas explored and presented in a text.

Third person: third person singular is "he/ she/ it" and plural is "they" – authors often write novels in the third person.

Tone: literally the sound of a text – How words sound (either in the mouth of an actor or the head of a reader) can crucially affect meaning/

Tragic: King Richard III and Macbeth are both murderous tyrants, yet only Macbeth is a *tragic* figure. Why? Because Macbeth has the potential to be great, recognizes the error he has made and all that he has lost in making it, and dies bravely in a way that seems to accept the justice of the punishment.

Graphic Organizer –plot

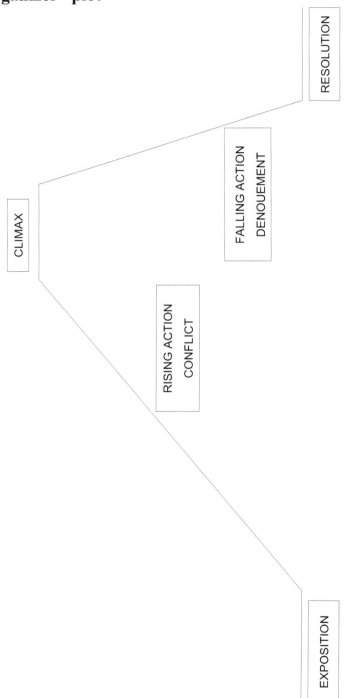

Graphic Organizer- perspectives

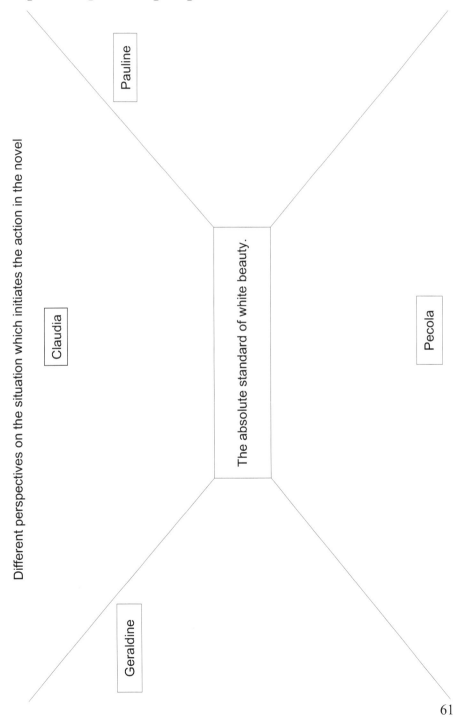

Different perspectives on the situation which initiates the action in the novel

Pauline

Claudia

The absolute standard of white beauty.

Pecola

Geraldine

How I Used the Study Guide Questions

Although there are both closed and open questions in the Study Guide, very few of them have simple, answers. They are designed to encourage in-depth discussion, disagreement, further research, and (eventually) consensus. Above all, they aim to encourage students to go to the text to support their conclusions and interpretations.

I am not so arrogant as to presume to tell you how to use this resource. I used it in the following ways, each of which ensured that students were well prepared for class discussion and presentations. They are described below:

1. Set a reading assignment and tell everyone to be aware that the questions will be the focus of whole class discussion the next class.

2. Set a reading assignment and allocate particular questions to sections of the class (e.g. if there are four questions, divide the class into four sections, etc.). In class, form discussion groups containing one person who has prepared each question and allow time for feedback within the groups. Have feedback to the whole class on each question by picking a group at random to present their answers and to follow up with class discussion.

3. Set a reading assignment, but do not allocate questions. In class, divide students into groups and allocate to each group one of the questions related to the reading assignment the answer to which they will have to present formally to the class. Allow time for discussion and preparation.

4. Set a reading assignment, but do not allocate questions. In class, divide students into groups and allocate to each group one of the questions related to the reading assignment. Allow time for discussion and preparation. Now reconfigure the groups so that each group contains at least one person who has prepared each question and allow time for feedback within the groups.

5. Before starting to read the text, allocate specific questions to individuals or pairs. (It is best not to allocate all questions to allow for other approaches and variety. One in three questions or one in four seems about right.) Tell students that they will be leading the class discussion on their question. They will need to start with a brief presentation of the issued and then conduct question and answer. After this, they will be expected to present a brief review of the discussion.

6. Having finished the text, or part thereof, arrange the class into groups of 3, 4 or 5. Tell each group to select as many questions from the Study Guide as there are members of the group. Each individual is responsible for drafting out a written answer to one question, and each answer should be a substantial paragraph. Each group as a whole is then responsible for discussing, editing and

suggesting improvements to each answer, which is revised by the original writer and brought back to the group for a final proof reading followed by revision. (This seems to work best when the group knows that at least some of the points for the activity will be based on the quality of all of the answers.)

To the Reader

Ray strives to make his texts the best that they can be. If you have any comments or question about this book *please* contact the author through his email: **moore.ray1@yahoo.com**
Visit his website http://www.raymooreauthor.com

Also by Ray Moore:

Books are available from amazon.com and from barnesandnoble.com as paperbacks and some from online eBook retailers.

Fiction:

The Lyle Thorne Mysteries

Each book features five mysteries from the Golden Age of Detection:

Investigations of The Reverend Lyle Thorne
Further Investigations of The Reverend Lyle Thorne
Early Investigations of Lyle Thorne
Sanditon Investigations of The Reverend Lyle Thorne
Final Investigations of The Reverend Lyle Thorne
Lost Investigations of The Reverend Lyle Thorne

Non-fiction:

The *Critical Introduction series*

This is written for high school teachers and students and for college undergraduates. Each volume gives an in-depth analysis of a key text:

"The Stranger" by Albert Camus: A Critical Introduction (Revised Second Edition)
"The General Prologue" by Geoffrey Chaucer: A Critical Introduction
"Pride and Prejudice" by Jane Austen: A Critical Introduction
"The Great Gatsby" by F. Scott Fitzgerald: A Critical Introduction

The Text and Critical Introduction series

This differs from the Critical introduction series as these books contain the original text and in the case of the medieval texts an interlinear translation to aid the understanding of the text. The commentary allows the reader to develop a deeper understanding of the text and themes within the text.

"Sir Gawain and the Green Knight": Text and Critical Introduction
"The General Prologue" by Geoffrey Chaucer: Text and Critical Introduction
"The Wife of Bath's Prologue and Tale" by Geoffrey Chaucer: Text and Critical Introduction
"Heart of Darkness" by Joseph Conrad: Text and Critical Introduction
"The Sign of Four" by Sir Arthur Conan Doyle Text and Critical Introduction
"A Room with a View" By E.M. Forster: Text and Critical Introduction

The Bluest Eye by Toni Morrison

"Oedipus Rex" by Sophocles: Text and Critical Introduction
"Henry V" by William Shakespeare: Text and Critical Introduction
Study guides - listed alphabetically by author
* denotes also available as an eBook
NOTE Amazon has recently required Study Guides to reflect the nature of the book so eBooks are titled "Study Guide on …."

"ME and EARL and the Dying GIRL" by Jesse Andrews: A Study Guide
"Pride and Prejudice" by Jane Austen: A Study Guide
"Moloka'i" by Alan Brennert: A Study Guide
"Wuthering Heights" by Emily Brontë: A Study Guide*
"Jane Eyre" by Charlotte Brontë: A Study Guide *
"The Myth of Sisyphus" by Albert Camus: A Study Guide
"The Stranger" by Albert Camus: A Study Guides
"The Myth of Sisyphus" and "The Stranger" by Albert Camus: Two Study Guides *
Study Guide to "Death Comes to the Archbishop" by Willa Cather
"The Awakening" by Kate Chopin: A Study Guide
"The Meursault Investigation" by Kamel Daoud: A Study Guide
Study Guide on "Great Expectations" by Charles Dickens *
"The Sign of Four" by Sir Arthur Conan Doyle: A Study Guide *
"The Wasteland, Prufrock and Poems" by T.S. Eliot: A Study Guide
"The Great Gatsby" by F Scott Fitzgerald: A Study Guide
"A Room with a View" by E. M. Forster: A Study Guide
"Looking for Alaska" by John Green: A Study Guide
"Paper Towns" by John Green: A Study Guide
Study Guide to "Catch-22" by Joseph Heller *
"Unbroken" by Laura Hillenbrand: A Study Guide
"The Kite Runner" by Khaled Hosseini: A Study Guide
"A Thousand Splendid Suns" by Khaled Hosseini: A Study Guide
"Go Set a Watchman" by Harper Lee: A Study Guide
"On the Road" by Jack Keruoac: A Study Guide
"Life of Pi" by Yann Martel: A Study Guide *
Study Guide on "The Invention of Wings" by Sue Monk Kidd *
"The Secret Life of Bees" by Sue Monk Kidd: A Study Guide
"Esperanza Rising" by Pam Munoz Ryan: A Study Guide
"Animal Farm" by George Orwell: A Study Guide
Study Guide on "Nineteen Eight-Four" by George Orwell
Study Guide to "Selected Poems" by Sylvia Plath *
"An Inspector Calls" by J.B. Priestley: A Study Guide
"The Catcher in the Rye" by J.D. Salinger: A Study Guide
"Where'd You Go, Bernadette" by Maria Semple: A Study Guide
"Henry V" by William Shakespeare: A Study Guide

*Study Guide on "Macbeth" by William Shakespeare ***
*"Othello" by William Shakespeare: A Study Guide ***
*"Antigone" by Sophocles: A Study Guide ***
"Oedipus Rex" by Sophocles: A Study Guide
"Cannery Row" by John Steinbeck: A Study Guide
"East of Eden" by John Steinbeck: A Study Guide
*"Of Mice and Men" by John Steinbeck: A Study Guide**
*Study Guide to "The Grapes of Wrath" by John Steinbeck: ***
"The Goldfinch" by Donna Tartt: A Study Guide
"Walden; or, Life in the Woods" by Henry David Thoreau: A Study Guide
Study Guide to "Cat's Cradle" by Kurt Vonnegut
*"The Bridge of San Luis Rey" by Thornton Wilder: A Study Guide ***
A Study Guide on "The Book Thief" by Markus Zusak

Study Guides available as e-books:

A Study Guide on "Heart of Darkness" by Joseph Conrad:
A Study Guide on "The Mill on the Floss" by George Eliot
A Study Guide on "Lord of the Flies" by William Golding
A Study Guide on "Nineteen Eighty-Four" by George Orwell
A Study Guide on "Henry IV Part 2" by William Shakespeare
A Study Guide on "Julius Caesar" by William Shakespeare
A Study Guide on "The Pearl" by John Steinbeck
A Study Guide on "Slaughterhouse-Five" by Kurt Vonnegut

New titles are added regularly.

Teacher resources:

Ray also publishes many more study guides and other resources for classroom use on the 'Teachers Pay Teachers' website:

http://www.teacherspayteachers.com/Store/Raymond-Moore

Made in the USA
Middletown, DE
03 June 2020